The Widowhood Explosion

WIDOWHOOD in the 21st century

Helen Wolfers

Melbourne, Australia

Helen Wolfers c/- Intertype
Unit 45, 125 Highbury Road
BURWOOD VIC 3125
www.intertype.com.au

Book Layout ©2019 www.intertype.com.au

Ordering Information:
Quantity sales. Special discounts are available on quantity purchases by corporations, associations and others. For details, contact the "Special Sales Department" at the address above.

Dead Men's Wives – Helen Wolfers
ISBN 978-0-6485960-7-3

'widowhood needs to be re-invented both for those who live it and those who fear it.'

Genevieve Davis Ginsberg (New York Times, 1987)

CONTENTS

Preface

Today 80% of all married women in the most technologically advanced countries can expect to outlive their husbands, many for as long as twenty years! If, as Shakespeare said, there are seven stages in the lives of men, for women of the modern Western world there is now an eighth – widowhood.

For a variety of reasons there have always been more widows than widowers in most societies, but in the latter half of the twentieth century the prevalence and duration of widowhood increased dramatically.

An experience as common and prolonged as this must be considered a normal phase of women's lives. Yet, despite the current explosion of interest in women's issues, the subject of widowhood is conspicuous only by its absence. Widows are still without representation and they have no role in society. They are stereotyped, marginalised, virtually invisible in the media and almost totally untapped as a target in the consumer market. Even the leaders of the Women's Movement itself have not addressed anything more than a passing reference to this subject, despite the fact that gender discrimination has affected widows no less than any other category of women. The cause of every conceivable minority group has by now been championed, but not the widows.

As sexually experienced women without male partners, widows throughout the ages were often seen as a threat to the social order and because of their close association with death, widows are still today in modern society also a menacing reminder of what most of us would rather forget. These two major associations of the widow with sex and death, have made her a prime target for metaphorising, demonising and ostracising throughout history.

Two social changes in the post-industrial Western world have greatly affected modern widowhood. The first was the elevation of marriage in the 19th century to the only desirable status for women and the second, the replacement of sex by death as the great taboo of the 20th century. These two factors have combined to alienate widows still further. While widows are today economically more independent than ever before, they are also lonelier and more marginalised than ever before. With full inheritance rights and widows' pensions, they are no longer in physical danger of annihilation as many were in former times. But they are still socially degraded and this fall from grace has been made even more poignant for modern widows because of the exaggerated importance that was attached to marriage and motherhood in the industrial and post-industrial eras from which these women have emerged.

There is great variation in the experience of widowhood. Women who have remained in the workforce after having children will be better equipped to face widowhood than those who did not. As the next generation of widows will contain a far higher proportion of such women, they can be expected to fare better on this score. Similarly, many of the gender related problems of present-day widowhood such as managing household finances, fixing appliances, etc., are likely to disappear or at least diminish in the future.

The experience of widowhood will vary greatly for those who still have dependent children to raise and those who don't. For these, or others caught unprepared for the loss of a spouse's disability pension or some other financial consequence of spousal bereavement, finances are likely to loom high on the agenda of problems in widowhood. And for women who are among the first

in a social circle to become widows the negative social consequences of widowhood will be far more severe than for those who
lose their husbands when most of their friends are already widows.
Depending upon the type of relationship in the marriage the loss
of physical protection or a sexual partner may be one of paramount
importance in widowhood. Loneliness is the biggest problem for
many, but not all, widows.

But almost all widows, rich and poor, educated and unedu-
cated, young and old, strong and weak, complain of being marginalised by society. Widows in all walks of life complain about their
subjective feelings of denigration and loss of status, to each other,
in widow-to-widow groups, on the Widownet and in their books.
It is for this reason that this book targets this problem of modern
widowhood with greater emphasis than any of its other psychological or social consequences.

Some of today's widows (aged 60-80) were the very women
who, 50 years ago, pioneered the post-war Women's Liberation
Movement that has transformed the lives of their daughters. These
were the women who, in the sixties and seventies, participated in
consciousness-raising sessions across the Western world and then
went on to achieve a Bill of Rights which gave their daughters the
freedom to choose what to be apart from wives and mothers and,
eventually, widows. And now, these same women are the widows
who today hover impotently on the fringes of society, caught between an order that is passing and one that has not yet arrived.

CHAPTER 1

Introduction

I awoke to the first day of my widowhood as though it were the first day of a terminal illness. In the reactions of those around me I sensed that I had been diminished as by some chronic disease – a condition from which I thought I would never again be free, for the rest of my life.

Widowhood is the most devastating experience to befall a 'normal' human life. It is accorded the highest score in questionnaires designed to measure stress (Holmes & Rahe, 1967). It has certainly been the most devastating event of my life.

Nonetheless there have been moments when I have felt that I would not have missed this part of my life for worlds; moments when I have felt exhilarated at having survived this ordeal intact. To triumph over an experience as searing as this does not come lightly. I know that I am more sensitive, more compassionate and stronger than ever I was before widowhood. In many ways, I am a better person as a widow than I was as a wife and my great regret is that David, my husband, cannot be here now to see how I have grown.

Marriage partners nurture each other, feed into each other's needs in a myriad of ways of which we are often unaware. When one dies, the prop is kicked from under the other's feet. The surviving partner must find new ways to define herself (and it is 'her' in 80% of marriages), new ways to satisfy the needs formerly met in marriage. Yet, this experience, while extremely painful, can also be creative and exhilarating, a new challenge to fill our extending years of life.

I was among the first of my social circle to be widowed. My husband was 67 when he died. I was 62 and had not yet fully registered that we were no longer young. When he died, I couldn't grasp that it was all over so quickly – it had gone by in a flash.

When I reached the stage of reflecting on our vanished lives together, the mathematics of what had been, might have been and, perhaps, should have been began invading my mind. I had had just under half of my life with him. I had never stopped along the road to consider how long we would be together – just took it for granted that we would be together forever. Somehow, widowhood is never thought about as part of the life cycle; not in our thoughts, not in our culture and hardly in our literature.

Then came the regrets. We should have had at least another decade together. However, the thought did occur and very forcibly, that had I been ten years older when I was widowed, I'd have had much less chance of creating the new life that I so obviously had to create now.

But then another somewhat startling thought crossed my mind. I hesitate to air it without first affirming that I would never ever, never in a million years, choose to become a widow. Nevertheless, being now widowed and having now learnt the very deep lesson that happiness is appreciation of what one has and unhappiness the appreciation of what one had, the thought came to me that ten more years with my husband would have just been ten more years of the same – comfortable patterns that we had acquired through 30 years of interdependence. Becoming a widow throws you out of the comfort-zone; confronts you with new problems – some terrible indeed; throws up your deepest fears and anxieties. But if you can succeed in staying the course, the rewards can be great. It can be, in the fullest sense, a born-again experience, a reawakening to an awareness which one last experienced only as a child.

To top this heretical thought which first occurred to me two and a quarter years after my husband's death, a close friend happened to say that very day that, in his opinion, many women flourish, come into their own, acquire a second lease on life once they overcome the initial devastating grief of widowhood.

Once I had regained my balance after the death of my husband, I felt, for the first time in my life, that nothing could defeat me. Rightly or wrongly, I felt that I had survived the worst that life could deal me. From such an experience, one can gain enormous self-confidence. A very large part of negotiating widowhood successfully is to learn to use this new-found source of self-confidence to counter the devastation to self-esteem being simultaneously meted out to new widows by society.

Widowhood launched me on an inward journey that I had never so profoundly experienced before. There were periods in my life when I had become more aware of my own feelings, about romantic love, religion, unreasonable hatreds, but never anything like this. For days on end, I found myself obsessed with my feelings and innermost thoughts about just about anything; marriage, widowhood, friends, life, death, children - I had, in short, become much more sensitive and aware, more analytic and in need of meaning. I became a more interesting person to myself. I assume now that most women, once widowed, have an added dimension gained through these soul-searing experiences and I see women who have been widowed as more sensitive and worldly-wise.

Widowhood is no new experience. But widowhood in the 21st. century, is changing more rapidly and more dramatically than ever before. From the biblical Ruth and Naomi, to Queen Victoria, Scarlet O'Hara and Jacqueline Kennedy, the type of widowhood women have experienced has been shaped by the economic, social and political conditions of the societies they inhabited. The current generation of widows was born in the 30's, 40's and 50's of the last century (widows begin to proliferate in their mid 60's). Women born in this era grew up in a society in which most still expected, as they had since biblical times, that their status and identity would be determined by the men they married. Wives still used their husbands first and surnames to identify themselves, e.g., Mrs. John Smith and Amy Vanderbilt's Complete Book of Etiquette published in 1954, still instructed widows to keep their husbands first name on their calling cards, even after his demise!

These women were amongst the first to achieve tertiary education in large numbers, but few were seriously pursuing careers. Whether filling in the years between school and marriage by learning a trade, studying for a degree or working for a wage, the overwhelming majority of young women still expected to marry, have children and be supported for the rest of their lives by their future husbands. To work or pursue a career after becoming a mother was considered selfish and irresponsible.

The fact is that many women of this generation, though sexually liberated and highly educated - indeed, many were active in the Women's Liberation Movement of the sixties and seventies - were still nevertheless socially defined by their husbands and, when their husbands now die, they suffer a loss in status.

On September 17th 1994, I joined a group of over 30 million women in the Western world whose existence I had previously barely noticed. As I began my descent down the tortuous path of widowhood, I found it more and more incomprehensible that such a substantial sub-population (11 million in the USA, over a million in my country, Australia) should be drifting like flotsam and jetsam on the margins of society.

I have since met many widows who, as individuals, have succeeded admirably in negotiating the difficult transition to widowhood. I have also met many who haven't. But as a class widows remain disunited, unstudied and unrepresented.

Every widow has a unique story to tell, but once widowed, as a class they experience a loss in status common to them all. ***Widowhood is a great leveller of women.***

As background to this book, I have selected several relevant events from my own personal initiation into widowhood to recount here.

A few months before my husband died, I met an old acquaintance in the local lending library whom I had not seen for many years. Janette invited David and me to dinner. 'Allen will be thrilled to see you both again,' she said. I did not give what should have been the natural, immediate, truthful response: 'I'm sorry, but we can't come to supper. David is terminally ill with cancer. Perhaps you'd like to come and see him before he dies. He's not in any pain and mentally quite unaffected and receiving visitors every day'. Or: 'Perhaps after it's all over I could visit you and Alan and we'll catch up on the past a little then'.

Instead, I said, 'Thank you very much. We're a bit tied up just now, but I'll get back to you soon and we'll arrange something. Give me your telephone number'.

I went out, locked myself in the car and tried to fathom why I hadn't been able to tell her the truth, that David was dying. Part of it, no doubt, was the embarrassment it would have caused her. In the easiest of circumstances, anything to do with death and dying causes embarrassment to most people and this, compounded with the shock of such unexpected news, would no doubt have created a very awkward situation.

But I knew that that was not the whole of it - not even the most of it. I hadn't told her that David was dying, not for <u>her</u> sake to avoid embarrassment, but for mine, to protect <u>me</u> from something. I realised for the first time that I was ***ashamed*** of the fact that my husband was going to die.

But why was I ashamed? Why on God's earth should I feel shame for my terrible misfortune - self-pity, anger, guilt, practically any other emotion would have been more appropriate than shame.

It occurred to me also that I had retained an appearance, an identity that I was no longer entitled to. Janette had extended the dinner invitation on behalf of herself and her husband, as one couple to another and I had maintained the fiction that David and I were still a couple in the running for dinner invitations. That is what I had not been willing to cede. Instinctively I knew that, as a single person, I might not have been offered the invitation in the first place. I was a fraud. Perhaps that was what I was ashamed of.

As one thought led to another, I wondered why I would expect not to be invited to dinner without a husband to accompany me. Invitations to dinner parties were, amongst other things, a measure of one's social ranking. I had always been aware that who got invited where was very significant, but I had not, till this moment, consciously registered that widows normally didn't get invited to dinners for couples at all. I was now embarking on a social downgrading which I could do nothing to avoid. I realised for the first time that it would not matter how much status I had acquired as a woman by career or wealth; the humblest married woman would now have a standing in society that I was about to lose. I felt panicked and nauseated as it dawned on me that, society would henceforth view me as something less than I had been.

In retrospect, I realise that I, myself, must have subconsciously regarded widows as second-class women. Why else would I be feeling shame at the prospect of becoming one?

Prompted by my unexpected reaction to this incident, I began for the first time to try to envisage myself as a widow. I decided to ask a real widow about how her life had changed with the death of her husband, so I telephoned a friend who had been widowed two years previously and we arranged to meet for coffee. We started by exchanging inconsequential pleasantries, avoiding the subject uppermost in my mind. Then I explained why I had called her. Suddenly, her face clouded over:

'Your world is coming to an end', she said, then added, 'and it's not a nice club you're about to join'.

With this broken sentence, I had been admitted to 'the club' - it was my initiation. It was the first time I had been spoken to widow-to-widow. From that day, I learnt that widows form a closed club and there are things they say within that club that they don't say outside of it. I learnt later that there are two distinct reasons for this, both frequently articulated and analysed within the 'club'. One is that people who have not been through what we have simply do not understand what we're talking about - they might not believe us, they might ridicule us, they might think us paranoid. The other is that it is counter-productive to show our misery and weaknesses to other people as they will only shun us all the more.

This was my first insight into how a great many new widows in my environment felt - completely transformed, wiped out and destroyed. Children learn to understand the world through the reactions of those about them who have already been through the experience and this is how I was being conditioned to understand the widowhood ahead of me: 'Your world is coming to an end and it's not a nice club you're about to join'. I broke into a cold sweat.

There were several subliminal messages in that one sentence:

- that the lives of my generation of women had been totally defined by their relationship to their husbands.

- that with David's demise this world as I knew it would disappear and with it the self I had hitherto been.

- that widows might not simply be women whose husbands had died, but a class which automatically became members of a club without their initiative or consent.

- that this club that I was about to join willy-nilly was 'not nice'.

I had never before thought of widows as belonging to a club. The discovery startled me, as had the revelation of my impending loss of status and my first experience of shame. They were a series of shock waves, buffeting me into a new image of myself as a widow, initiation rites for entry into the 'club'.

During the four months that I knew David was going to die, I did a lot of crying and screaming, usually on my own in the car. But as the reality of what was going to happen gradually sank in, fear - stark naked fear - began to override every other emotion. When my husband did die, I was terrified. My initial response to bereavement was terror, not grief. The grief came later.

I had never been that terrified before. During those terrible first weeks, I would awake in cold sweats, my hair standing on end as the skin of my scalp contracted. My heart would thump with panic. I remember reading the description by a Holocaust survivor of his physiological reactions when he first realised that all the Jews in his town were going to die. They seemed to be the same as those I was experiencing now.

I have since learnt that this is not an uncommon experience. Yet how many women know beforehand that this may be their initial reaction to widowhood? I have a university degree in psycho-pathology and still I did not know that terror rather than grief might be my first reaction to David's death. How much better might I have coped had I been prepared and given guidance on how to deal with the panic of terror? Just knowing that it could happen or, indeed, was even likely to happen, would have reduced the impact. Surprisingly, terror is not normally considered as part of the syndrome of bereavement. As it was, I was left to deal with it alone.

We had a very close friend called Sam, a specialist in cancer research, who had come from the United States to Australia to be with us while David was dying. I soon found that by holding close to him after David died, I could subdue the terror. I knew this was sick and had to be fought from the onset. I would cling to him for days, then try to go for a walk alone, consciously increasing the time away from him each day.

The first walk away was a nightmare. Sam had taken me to a small seaside resort for a few days after the funeral. It was a brilliant sunlit day. Life was stirring in the streets - shops opening, delivery vans bringing the new day's supplies to a country town, fishermen out for an early catch, unwinding lines and nets and holiday makers jogging along the beach, a few already in the sea. Yet I felt as though I were on the moon - alone, silent, cold, in a grey vacuum. My skin prickled with fear and my head throbbed with pain. Each step was an almost impossible achievement. I concentrated on my feet, guiding one after the other like a child walking for the first time, or a double amputee taking her first steps on artificial limbs. Each step away from the motel room where Sam was still sleeping, increased the fear gripping my chest. I set myself a goal of reaching the corner shop to buy milk and bread and that released the tension and steadied my panic. It was a technique that I was to learn to use a great deal in the coming year: define the parameters, limit the goals, one step at a time.

Three years later while at San Francisco airport during a business trip to the United States, I was distracted by the sound of heavy sobbing behind me. I buried my head further into my morning newspaper and tried to ignore it. But as the sobs became louder and more anguished, I folded my paper and turned to see what was happening. There, under a stack of parcels and luggage, was a large black woman in a bright green taffeta dress with matching turban-like hat. I sat down beside her, took her hand and asked what was wrong. She told me that her husband was critically ill in the Veterans' Hospital in Washington. She was on her way to see him for the last time. As I drew closer to her to give her a sympathetic hug I was repelled by the smell of alcohol. Then, just as I was about to pull back her eyes caught mine and just for a spilt second I saw in them the panic and terror of impending widowhood. I realised in that split second that this was the first time I had found real communion with another human being since David had died.

Although fear and panic were my overriding reactions to David's death, these were interspersed with the pain of grief and, to my astonishment, an enormous appetite for sex. My appetite for food had, incidentally, disappeared altogether and I learnt in the first two weeks after David died that one could go without food for days without feeling hunger.

I found a ready and willing partner in Sam to gratify my erotic reaction. What began as a solace and a comfort to us both soon fanned itself into an uncontrollable lust with a will of its own and we found ourselves returning to the motel every few hours. Sex gave us both transitory relief from acute grief and that in itself was enormously rewarding. In my research for this book, I have since come across several references to reported heightened sexuality in the early days of widowhood. I have also observed it for myself in group support sessions, where widows say things to one another that they hide from the outside world.

In those hellish first weeks, I found in sex the only wholesome relief from pain; it was better than pills and had no adverse side effects. Freud examined the relationship between death and sex in his essay Thanatos and Eros. It has long been known to writers and artists. But I had never visualised it as the crude and immediate reaction to bereavement that I was now experiencing. I swung from the depths of despair to manic elation, high on sex!

It took me the mandatory two years to overcome my grief. As all the textbooks tell us, there is great variation in how people deal with grief, but two years is the most commonly agreed norm and, of course, it doesn't just go away one day. But for most people it gradually recedes and so it did for me.

But the further my grief receded, the more I became aware of my new marginalisation in society. I began to feel it in everything - in every encounter, in every activity, every hour of the day and even in my bed at night. I became aware to what extent David and I had formed a social unit and now that this unit had ruptured I found myself adrift in a territory in which all the old familiar boundaries had suddenly been redrawn. Now there were social interactions that I could no longer be part of, no matter how successful a career woman, how scintillating a person, how loving or generous or kind - and all because I was no longer part of a couple.

When I was still a married woman, I had taken for granted the status that this bestowed upon me. A married woman, even in a bad marriage, holds a privileged identity in society, the advantages of which I only felt with its loss. My friends found it difficult to believe my vehement insistence that I felt demeaned because I was no longer a married woman. My apparent self-confidence and competence belied it.

But it has little to do with confidence or competence. In many ways, I became more confident and certainly more self-reliant after David died. He was a highly educated man, more knowledgeable than I. I looked up to him, relied on his judgement and accepted his advice in most things, but after his death I had to take over the management of our extensive investments scattered over several continents. Within a year I was comfortable in my new role as sole director of our companies. If anything, I was financially better off as a widow than a wife, as my income had not dropped and there was now only one consumer instead of two.

Still, every little thing I did or thought or felt in the first months after David died was somehow related to this assault on my self-esteem. Filling the car with gas, collecting the mail, writing the cheques, programming the answering machine ('I' instead of 'we' 'cannot come to the phone right now'); shopping, washing, cooking for one was somehow pathetic.

I remember once having to drive myself home from hospital after a minor operation because David had an important business engagement and thinking nothing of it. Now I was desolate if a friend did not come to collect me in similar circumstances. Driving yourself home after a minor operation, when your husband is alive is displaying a degree of toughness and bravado. But when you are a widow it is because you are alone, unloved and belong to no one.

I realised some years later that what had been so difficult for me at first was overcoming my own (and society's) image of females as passive, recipient and protected. In widowhood, I was forced to choose between becoming totally independent or totally dependent, the habitual giver or the habitual receiver, the helper or the helpless. There was no longer any middle path. Choosing independence translated, in my mind, to mean 'no one cares for me anymore; I belong to no one now; I am no longer worthy of anyone's protection. Hence, I am not a real woman anymore'.

Strangely enough, I felt this loss of self-esteem as much when I was alone and there was no one there to see my pathos as when I was with others. It made no difference if the gas station was busy or empty when I pulled in to fill my tank. In fact, I think in retrospect it was all the more pitiful if there was only me. To sit in an empty restaurant alone was even more pathetic than to be part of a crowd.

Nowhere was I more disoriented and convulsed by my return to singledom than in the privacy of my own bed. I had absolutely no image of who I was and what was now expected of me as a sexual being. I did not know or even think about what was going to happen to my sex life, nor at that point did I care. What bothered me was that I did not know what I was expected to want or how I was expected to behave. I did not know what people thought about women who went to bed alone, night after night, perhaps for the rest of their lives. I did not even know where to put myself; it took me a year to leave the side I had always occupied when there were two of us in the bed.

A couple of months after David died, a well-meaning friend asked if I'd like to meet an eligible man.

'Yes, sure', I said a little dazed, not yet having returned in my mind, to the idea of socialising again.

'He's intelligent, good-looking and a wonderful person, but he's not Jewish. Does that bother you?'

'No, should it?' I asked. What was I going to do with him anyway that his religion should affect me, one way or another?

The man, let's call him John (in fact I have forgotten his real name), was on the phone within the hour. Had all this happened a year later my reaction may have been very different. I had not yet had time to understand the singles scene of the third age. I did not yet realise the enormity of the imbalance between the sexes, available single women out-numbering single men by about ten to one from any quick count at a bridge club, on a tour bus or in a retirement village. I had not yet witnessed the undignified scramble for any new widower or divorced man. I had not yet heard of the desperate widows, crazed by loneliness, who pursue available men, even those with one foot already in the grave. I had not yet witnessed, as I was to a year later, widows putting their names and addresses into the pockets of a new widower at his wife's funeral 'in case he needed their help'.

Had I had but an inkling of the new social scene I was about to enter I might not have viewed poor John, racing enthusiastically up the front garden path, flowers in hand, with such utter shock and contempt.

'He's old enough to be my grandfather!', I thought. I was dismayed to see this old man, in his late sixties or early seventies, coming to collect me for a date. The last time a man had picked me up for a date was when I was about twenty and he no more than twenty-three. In my subconscious mind, that was what I was expecting - maybe a man of forty-five or fifty. But seventy! At seventy you no longer brought flowers or dated!

I went to coffee with him in shock. Slowly he came into focus and when I'd calmed down enough, I managed a flickering glimmer of perspective on myself. I was now a woman of sixty-two. David was sixty-seven when he died. In my mind he was still the 30- year-old I had married. I realised then and there whilst drinking coffee with John that this was going to take a great deal more thinking through and adjusting to, than minding if he were Jewish or not. In retrospect, he was, or certainly seemed to be on first acquaintance, an intelligent, gentle and not bad looking septuagenarian. What's more, he was a psychiatrist, a man of means, with a lovely home. Quite a catch on the seniors' scene today. Which would have soon brought me to the next question: 'How come he was still available after several years of divorce?' Something must be wrong, but I didn't return to find out.

I remember the anxiety, as a teenager, of being between boyfriends. Not having a boyfriend meant that there was something wrong with you, that you were ugly or unpopular, not as desirable as those girls who had boyfriends and, most important of all, you had no-one to partner you on outings. There was a mad dash to exit this state of limbo between relationships as quickly as possible and who one achieved this with was often of secondary importance.

What I was experiencing now in my return to singledom was, in part at least, a resurgence of these teen-age anxieties. But what was a solution at eighteen, even if flawed and inappropriate, was not possible at sixty. One cannot solve the problems of singleness in widowhood by getting a man. Firstly, there aren't enough to go round and secondly the most probable outcome will be widowhood again within a few short years. ***Being single after marriage is a very different experience to being single before it.***

When I became a widow, I was also suddenly released not only from my marriage vows, but also from my commitments to a partnership. Suddenly, I didn't have to be home by any given time at night without calling to say where I was. There was no-one to call. I didn't have to be home at all. I didn't have to plan anything to suit anyone – not a meal, not a trip, nothing.

I felt elation in my new freedom, particularly after the last few years of strain and worry over David's illness. But I also felt cut adrift, I vacillated between wanting to fly into the unknown and crawl back into the womb. I missed my mother again after not having thought about her for a decade.

My first demonstration of independence to myself was my decision was to have a face-lift. This was something that David had absolutely forbidden. My face had become ravaged by the worries of the last few years. The results of the procedure were dramatic and helped me a great deal in the eventual struggle to regain my self-esteem. But there were other, less obvious, advantages. It gave me a purpose and a focus in the first few months of bereavement. I undertook extensive research into the medical and financial aspects of the procedure, comparing the pros and cons of the different techniques available and, above all, the competence of the various surgeons. Once I had made my choice, I surrendered myself entirely to his care and this was a very comforting experience at that time. The actual pain after the operation was also a plus. It distracted my attention away from the psychological pain of bereavement. I learnt from my surgeon that a substantial proportion of his clients were newly bereaved widows.

My new sexual freedom was not as easy to deal with. The first weeks of frantic sex with Sam had not demanded any decision-making on my part. I was in a state of shock, responding reflexively to those about me, like a patient emerging from anesthesia. But even after I began to put my life together again in other ways, my sexuality as a widow remained a problem.

On the rare occasions in my life that I have gone to a synagogue, I would pass the time looking down from the women's gallery above at the impressive array of outstanding leaders of the community in the front rows. The most prestigious judges, politicians and doctors looked somehow elemental, almost babyish in their striped ceremonial shawls and this association had the strange effect of making me visualise them in bed, the blue and white striped shawls becoming the bed linen. Now, as a widow, I found myself visualising them as sexual partners and the idea appalled me.

I came to the conclusion that men of my generation were simply no longer sexually appealing to me except, perhaps, those I had known since I was young, because somehow in the old man I still saw the youth that I had once known, just as I had still seen David as a young man because we had aged together. I decided that I could probably bring myself to have an affair with a man near seventy if I had known him through the years, but as all the men I had known since youth were married, there was no one I could have sex with now. I would just have to forget it.

But as I began to engage again with the world around me, I discovered that other people had also invented theories about their evolving sexuality by which they rationalise the way they live. As a wife I had been less aware of them. As a widow, I was sexually deprived and available and so I became far more sensitive to the sexual undercurrents swirling around me. I was later to discover that the proverbial wives' fear of widows was not altogether the fantasy I had earlier dismissed as nonsense.

During the first couple of years after I was widowed, I was sometimes introduced to or sought out by widowed or divorced men, but I soon decided that these were not for me. Perhaps it was too early for me to relate to other people intimately, but I did not find any of them attractive; perhaps because of the shortage of available men, not only to senior widows but also to middle age divorcees, any reasonably attractive unattached man of my generation would be looking for a partner considerably younger than himself. I set about forging new friendships with interesting women and rekindling old friendships with married couples. My friends became my new extended family. One way or another I always had people around me and with some I became intimate - not sexually but humanly.

Gradually the loss of intimacy which I had felt so acutely in the first couple of years after David died was diminished by a wider circle of family and friends. I was never lonely now; I had more people around me, more company if not quite the same companionship, than I had ever had before and I was reasonably happy with this new pattern of human relationships. The old pangs of pain and desolation for the loss of my husband had disappeared.

And then, only after two years had passed, a new phenomenon entered my life - married men with unsatisfactory sex lives. Their approach was like some well-rehearsed soap-opera; they all loved their wives and would never leave them, but for one reason or another they all had unsatisfactory sex lives. That was the basic theme - with all sorts of minor variations. One was physically repulsed by his wife's body. For another, sex had become physically painful for the woman. Another needed sex outside his marriage to overcome impotence with his wife. I couldn't understand why all these married men were suddenly coming on to me, why all together at the same time and why had I never before heard about this pandemic of good marriages with bad sex?

Some of these men were reasonably attractive unlike the widowed and divorced men I had encountered in the beginning. As usual, I repaired to my academic analytical training to explain this new turn of events. As a new grieving widow, I must have been a threat because what I had desperately wanted straight after David died was a man, any man, to fill his place. That would have been the last thing these married men, who loved their wives and would never leave them, would have wanted to get involved in. But by now I was far more relaxed and self-sufficient and probably no longer a threat to their marriages.

I was rather derisive of these pitiful stories and dismissed them as a new version of the bullshit I had heard from men all my life when trying for a quick lay. I was reminded of young men in my youth who had scared me into believing that once aroused, they would suffer permanent physical damage unless allowed to finish what we had begun. I hadn't the faintest intention of taking them seriously, although it was good to feel wanted again.

Then one day I found myself in a predicament of my own making. I had repeatedly told those friends who were forever exhorting me 'to find a man' that the only man I could imagine myself having an affair with now was one with whom I had had an affair, or at least had a crush on, when we were young. I had even named some of them jokingly, fully confident that the idea was only fantasy as they were all married. Then, by sheer accident, I met up with one of these men while on a business trip in the States. He told me how he had always known that I was sexually attracted to him, something I myself had not been consciously aware of, but on reflection now accepted as probably correct. He also told me that he had not slept with his wife for years and that they were both happy with that arrangement.

Here I was confronted with the exact situation that I had often cited as the sole set of circumstances in which I could envisage ever having sex again. Initially I resisted because he was married. But he persisted, protesting that this would not be a betrayal as I was not taking anything from anyone. I realised in that moment that I was damned if I did and damned if I didn't. Mercifully, I had never met his wife and my previous rationalisation for my celibacy as a widow was at stake. I gave way and slept with him.

That experience had a devastating effect on me. The day after I had slept with this man simply to comply with a theory I had evolved to guide myself through a perplexing situation, I found that those old long-forgotten emotions of romantic love were stirring within me. I was thinking of nothing else but him, longing for him, fearing the separation which would soon take him away. I awoke the next day in a deep depression, not because this could only ever be a frustrated love affair, but because I was suddenly questioning whether my whole life had also been determined by some similar psychological quirk. I saw through the cunning trick that nature plays on us: sleep with a man because you find him attractive, or because you need a partner for social approval, or to justify a theory and bingo, you're trapped in a web of romantic illusion.

Had my life with David and all this pain on losing him also been founded only on an illusion? Had I understood this thirty years ago, would my life have been different and this monumental experience of widowhood never have happened? I knew the whole idea was nonsense but nonetheless it unsettled me. Ever since David's death, I had been very aware of how emotionally labile I had become. Anything that did not go according to plan, even a postponed appointment, could send me into depression. I knew that this was a natural consequence of grief but I had learnt to fear these swings of mood. I knew that this new irrational doubt, if unresolved, could send me into another period of depression.

To try to get a grip on my emotions. I decided to sleep with this man again. I wanted to experience the encounter once more, fully conscious of what was happening and in control of myself. I wanted to outwit nature, to enjoy the experience as a mature woman in control of her own destiny; nothing more and nothing less.

The next day I realised that, for the first time since he had died, I hadn't thought about David for a whole day. In a way this experience marked my final separation from him and acceptance of widowhood as a discrete new phase in my life, with as much potential as any other that I had passed through before.

My initiation into widowhood was in many ways benign. I was supported by friends and children. I have not suffered economically and I came to it with a strong and self-assertive personality. And still I found the experience shattering. Not the grief, which was devastating but expected, normal and surmountable. It was the social impact that was so crippling and intractable. If this was so for one as privileged in widowhood as I was, how much more so must it be for those who are not?

The advice often given to widows is to 'remake' themselves. 'To be happy in widowhood a woman must reinvent herself', the bereavement counsellors tell us. I have now met many widows who have reinvented themselves: they are courageous, successful, productive women. But usually they add a rider when asked to describe their new lives: 'My life is as good as it can be but there's still something missing' or; 'I've done all right, but somehow I'm never *really* happy anymore'.

This appears to have been the frame of mind of widows since the dawn of human history. Homer characterised the anticipation of widowhood in his play Andromede in much the same tone: 'When I am bereft of you' andromede said to her warrior husband on the eve of his departure for battle, 'it would be better for me to pass beneath the earth. There will be no more comfort for me only grief'.

Three thousand years later we still have a situation in which many widows are at best never really happy and at worst just waiting for the end. I cannot accept this as the best we can do. Anything as universal and prolonged as widowhood now is must be regarded as a natural phase of women's lives, to be lived to the full. Anything less is a waste of human potential and human resources.

Obviously, widows reinventing themselves is not ever going to be enough. ***Widowhood is a social problem and society, too, must change to allow widows to achieve their full potential.***

In addition to trying to reinvent myself, I decided to examine what was wrong with society and how to change it.

CHAPTER 2

There have always been widows

Since heterosexual bonding has always been a part of human civilisations, widowhood has probably always been a part of the human experience. Although until the present century, men normally lived longer than women, widows have, nevertheless, usually outnumbered widowers throughout history. This happened because in most cultures remarriage was encouraged for men but not for women. But during the last hundred years, the situation has reversed and women now live longer than men. Consequently, the excess of widows over widowers has steadily grown.

That widowhood was essentially women's business since the earliest times, is also supported by the fact that, contrary to normal practice in the English language, the feminine form *widow* is the base from which the masculine form *widower* was derived. Amazingly the masculine form only entered the language in the fourteenth century.

Biblical times

The care of widows appears to have been an important concern in ancient times. The ancient texts dealing with widows, notably the Code of Hammurabi and the Hebrew and Christian Bibles, place much importance on the responsibility of surviving male relatives - sons, stepsons, sons-in-law, fathers-in-law, brothers-in-law to care for widows,

Four thousand years ago, Hammurabi, the first emperor of ancient Babylon, formulated detailed laws concerning the provision of food and shelter for widows. For example, referring to widows who were not the only wife of the deceased husband, it was decreed that 'she may live in the house belonging to one of her sons if she chooses' to do so or, if she has no sons, in the house of one of her deceased husband's sons by another wife and that her husband's sons 'shall enter into a bond for her' to provide her with food and drink 'as a bride' or a 'daughter-in-law whom they love'. Well may today's widow envy such loving emotional support in her bereavement.

Hammurabi goes to great lengths to set out rules for every conceivable combination of circumstance, such as the widow who remains in her late husband's home, the one who chooses to return to her father's house and so on.

In ancient Israel, widows were amongst the most vulnerable members of society. Care of widows and orphans was forced by religious injunction onto the male next-of-kin and in the absence of close relatives, onto the community. Because of their total dependence, the physical lot of widows and orphans throughout history was usually deplorable, human greed being what it is. This undoubtedly accounts for the strong emphasis on their protection in the Judeo-Christian tradition.

Economically, the widow was reduced to total dependency unless the bride-price was substantial enough to support her. Of all the matrimonial property, only the bride-price remained the woman's inheritance and on the husband's death Rabbinic law granted priority to her claim to it over all other claimants. Legal custody of all other property from the marriage, including the children, went to male relatives of the husband. The abuse that this situation engendered is apparent from the detailed attention given to abuse of widows and orphans in the Bible: 'Blessed is he who cares for widows, cursed is he who does not'. The penalty for afflicting the widow or orphan was death at God's own hand so that the wives and children of such offenders 'shall themselves become widows and orphans'(Exodus 22:24). God and religion were invoked to feed these, the most vulnerable of society and to protect their rights with all the might and fury of the Lord.

Like the texts of Hammurabi, the Hebrew Bible delivers specific instructions for the provision of food and shelter for widows and orphans (Deuteronomy 14:28,29 and 24:19,20,21). The widow was a vulnerable dependent on society, fed along with the orphan and the 'stranger' (i.e. the homeless) from leftovers of the harvest. With no control over her deceased husband's property, her destiny must have been precarious to say the least. Remarkably, this was the fate of all widows irrespective of wealth and rank. *Widowhood was and still is in a different way, a great leveler of women*.

In both the Hebrew and Christian Bibles, although in quite different ways, the question of the status of widows is touched upon. The ancient Hebrew law governing the rights of widows was based on the principle that a woman rises to the status of her husband in life and should not descend from that level after his death. She is therefore entitled to be maintained by his heirs at the level she enjoyed as his wife. This is spelt out in detail as applying to clothing, residence, medical expenses and so on. Of particular interest is a directive that, while she is entitled to remain in the matrimonial home for the rest of her life, *to maintain her status*, she is not entitled to occupy the whole house as she is now alone and total occupation is not needed. Nor is she entitled to transfer occupancy to others or let the whole or part of it for financial gain, as the right of residency is solely in order to let her maintain *status*, not acquire profit. (Shulchan Aruch EH 94:1) Upon her death, the home reverts to the heirs of the husband. Nothing could be less unambiguously concerned with the maintenance of status as distinct from material provision. *It is awesome to realise that the loss of status suffered by a woman in transition from wife to widow was officially recognised as a social problem thousands of years ago, but not yet today.*

If a man died before fathering children, his eldest brother was obliged to marry his widow by religious injunction or, if there was no brother, some other male relative. It was the duty of the brother to impregnate the widow in order to ensure the continuance of the dead husband's line and the children thus born were considered to be the legal issue of the dead spouse, not the biological father. This custom, called Levirate marriage was intended to protect the dead husband's interests rather than his widow's, but nevertheless she gained protection from it. The brother became the provider for the widow, which must have been of great value to her. But the protection the widow gained by thus acquiring a new husband was in no part the purpose of Levirate marriage because it applied even when the next oldest brother was still a minor. The widow had to wait until he was old enough to impregnate her and was not free to find another husband to care for her in the meantime. (This practice could be viewed as the ancient equivalent of the modern technique of freezing a man's sperm for future use)

There is also an underlying implication of guilt and punishment associated with widows, but not of widowers in the Hebrew Bible. The city of Babylon, personified in the Bible as a woman, is threatened with widowhood in retribution for her sins (Isiah 47:9). Widowhood is punishment for the widow's sin. The Biblical story of

Yehuda and Tamar has left an enduring legacy of guilt to women who outlive their spouses. Tamar was first married to Yehuda's eldest son, Er. When Er died leaving her childless, by Levirate law she became the wife of Oran, Yehuda's next son. When Oran also died young, Yehuda, fearing that marriage to Tamar was somehow cursed, refused to allow her to be married to his last, youngest and only surviving son, Shelah, thereby defying Biblical law. To this day, Jewish folk-lore rejects marriage to a person twice widowed, male or female. The widow is responsible for her own widowhood!

The implication that widows are responsible for the deaths of their husbands was perpetuated in folklore, as in the Talmudic tale in which Huma, the widow of a deceased rabbi is suspected by the wife of a living rabbi of enticing her husband with her (Huma's) uncontrollable sexual emanations. The wife thereupon chased the widow away, swearing that she would stop her from 'killing *yet another man'* (Baskin, 1985).

Divorce was possible in Judaism but forbidden by Christian doctrine. For Christians, widowhood was the only escape from a bad marriage and still is today for practicing Catholics. ('What God has joined together, let no man put asunder'.) So for some Christian women, widowhood must have been a welcome release; and even for Jewish women, though divorce is lawful, it is necessary only for the husband, but not the wife, to consent to divorce. As some ultra- religious men in Israel today still veto divorce for years, sometimes until they die, even though they can and often do, go to prison for withholding consent unreasonably, it is possible that widowhood could have its upside amongst abused Hebrew wives as well.

In the Christian Bible, the status of the widow relates not to her relationship to her husband, but to God. During the first few centuries of the Christian era, widowhood was called the 'altar of

God'. Widows were considered to be the proteges of God and originally the Church undertook total responsibility for them. Having lost their earthly husbands, widows were assumed to be celibate and in Christian thought this was deemed to be purifying (in contrast to the Hebrew religion which considers celibacy an aberration). Christian widows were accordingly imbued with an aura of sanctity akin to nuns; widows having sublimated their carnal instincts in motherhood for the service of mankind and nuns, having repressed them in the service of God. Thus, the widow's social threat as an unattached female was resolved by stereotyping her as a sanctified celibate. In fact, rather than being seen as a threat, widows were believed to possess supernatural healing powers. They could thus live out the remainder of their lives as honoured members of society and not marginalised as a threat to it.

The early Church so extolled sexual abstinence that, by the beginning of the second century after Christ, a discreet 'state of virginity' was recognised by the Church. It granted those who practiced celibacy a special place of grace in God's affections. So important was this aspect of sexual abstinence of widowhood that 'widow' and 'virgin' eventually came to mean the same thing and one finds reference to virgins as widows and widows as virgins. Widowhood was exalted by the Church because sex in marriage was originally promoted as a necessary evil. In their eagerness to popularise the spiritual ideal of chastity, some theologians, notably St. Jerome (c. 400 AD) developed an image of women as insatiable and lecherous. Since married women were the ones concerned with the messy animalistic business of reproduction, entailing menstruation, pregnancy, birth and breast-feeding, they were viewed by the church as further removed from the state of grace than men. So in early Christian times, not only did women not have to suffer a diminution in social standing on becoming widowed, but were actually accorded higher status than married women.

The Church instituted a special role for widows - a rare occurrence indeed in the history of widowhood. This was the order of deacons, called Deaconia, first instituted to care for new converts to Christianity.

Later Deaconia developed as a service for widows, orphans, pilgrims, strangers and the poor. Female administrators of Deaconia, known as deaconesses, were originally mainly widows. Apart from caring for the needy, deaconesses also assisted priests in their sacral duties. Those widows who had been chosen as deaconesses achieved special status as a higher rank of widow distinguishing them from ordinary widows. *Not until the Middle Ages were widows again accorded a role in society and never again since then.*

From the earliest Christian times economic care of the widow had been the responsibility of the Church. At first, Paul, Jesus' disciple who was in charge widows' affairs, advised all widows not to re- marry, but was later forced to amend this to alleviate the growing burden on the Church. So now, on Paul's instructions, only older widows were to be exhorted not to remarry. He then created a new category of 'real widows' or 'widows indeed' i.e. widows with no male relatives. Only these widows were henceforth to receive Church aid. In the new Testament Christians were now instructed to 'give proper recognition to those widows who are really 'in need' (Timothy chapter 5 verse 1). The following verses begin to exhibit irritation with unwarranted advantage being taken of the Church: '... If the widow has children or grandchildren, these should learn to put their own their religion into practice by caring for their own family...'. So angry is the author at this deemed extortion of the Church that by verse 8 he is damning them as 'worse than unbelievers'! Verse 9 unambiguously defines who shall qualify henceforth as widows entitled to Church support as follows: no widow may be put on the list of widows unless she is over the age of 60, has been faithful to her husband, is well-known for good deeds, such as bringing up children, showing hospitality, washing the feet of the saints etc,. Younger widows were never to be put on such lists because when their sexual desires overcome their dedication to Christ they will want to remarry. And in any case apart from this, they will get into the habit of being idle, going from house to house (of loose morals) and not only will they become idlers, but low gossips and busybodies. Therefore, younger widows were counselled by the Church to remarry, (as the lesser of two evils).

The condition that widows must be over 60 to qualify for Church support practically cleared the Church of all further responsibility for widows, as people rarely reached the age of 60. (The same strategy was employed 1900 years later during the Great Depression when the American New Deal set the retirement pension age at 65, when average life expectancy was 60). In addition to this one is left wondering who, in the end, were the arbiters of her behaviour; who judged whether a widow had been a good enough Christian to qualify for the Church's support, which in fact could be life or death for her?

Officially the care of widows and their children remained the responsibility of a male relative or the Church for the next several hundred years. Without adequate protection widows were commonly abducted, raped and forced into unwanted marriages. Even though laws were expressly formulated to prohibit forced marriages of widows, nevertheless widows of wealthy families and royalty were manipulated into marriages to forge political and economic alliances right up until the end of the 19th century. And the lot of poor widows was, as always, far worse. Without Church or male protection women were forced into prostitution and crime and prison was often the only refuge.

The Middle Ages

The Middle Ages lasted for a thousand years. They are divided into two sectors: the early Middle Ages, also called the Dark Ages, which lasted from approximately 500 to 1100 AD and the late Middle Ages from 1100 to 1500 AD.

During this period the lives of widows underwent the most dramatic changes of any period in recorded history. The status of widowhood rose to a pinnacle toward the end of the Dark Ages which stands in stark contrast to the nadir it has reached in our present age.

An interesting comparison of the status of widows in the Middle Ages and today is that in both their elevation and depression, widows were the most extremely affected of all categories of women. That is, at the height of their social standing in the Middle Ages, widows were amongst the most empowered of all women's groups and at its depths in the 21st century, widows are amongst the most disempowered.

There are obviously variables peculiar to widowhood which necessitate that it be studied as a subject in its own right and not, as presently, accorded a cursory reference in articles on age and feminism.

The introduction of the feudal system had a major effect on the status of widows. It started in France in the 9th century and spread throughout Europe in the subsequent centuries, finally reaching England via the Norman conquest. Under this system, all land became the property of the king, his relatives or his appointed lords. It was then leased out to peasant families, often in perpetuity, in return for money or services, usually military. Inheritance of these permanent land leases was via males only. Women remained, as they had previously been, under the guardianship of some male member of the family.

While the bride brought to the marriage a dowry, which for the wealthy was usually land or money, for the poor clothing, furniture, etc. The groom brought a dower which was a type of insurance for his widow if he predeceased her. But in the event of her remarriage or death, the Dower usually reverted to the husband's family, thus remaining permanently in the bloodline.

Whereas previously, when a woman became a widow she had been under the guardianship of a male member of the family; now, she was able to inherit her husband's estate, which may have included a land lease. However, if she wished to remarry, she had to marry a man approved by the landlord or lose her ownership of the lease.

This practice was universal and opened the way to a whole new market in which the wardships of widows' estates could be traded. Suitors had to bid for the land- lord's approval of their marriages to widows which would enable them to take over the heiresses' estates for the rest of their lives. Alternatively, landlords would in some cases accept payment from widows for the right to choose their own husbands. But, on the new husband's death, the lease reverted to the male heir of the first deceased husband's bloodline. Thus, wardships were bought and sold like securities today.

Eventually the French king, Philip Augustus, modified the law so that land- lords could not marry off widows against their will unless their estates owed them unpaid dues, usually in military service. Finally, the power even of the king to sell the remarriages rights of widows was renounced by the Magna Carta in the thirteenth century. From the amount of recording and the eventual necessity for legislation to control it, this trade in wordships appears to have been big business from the 9th to the 11th centuries.

Under feudalism, both upper- and lower- class marriages were arranged to augment the land holdings of the families of the betrothed couple. Many people never married simply because there were not enough eligible landholding partners. Usually only the oldest son inherited land and so only he, of all his brothers, married.

Because so many men and women could never marry, prostitution was widely practiced and highly regulated. Both governments and Church disapproved in principle but tolerated it in practice (foreshadowing the attitude to the increasing acceptance of de-facto polygyny today in modern societies struggling with large excesses of unattached women). By this means, unmarried women of the lower classes were able to augment their meagre means from their conventional employment in domestic service and female labour on the land. On the other hand, unmarried girls of the aristocracy and wealthy merchant classes were often placed in convents which demanded hefty dowries for their admission. Interesting to note that in the Middle Ages society was forced to address the problems created by shortages of eligible males in the marriage market as we are still today in the 21st century.

Most widows worked, both on the land and in the towns, especially in the city craft industries where they were prominent in carrying on the family businesses. More than any other factor in medieval life, it was widows' participation in the workforce that was responsible for this becoming the *golden age of widowhood.*

With the development of the orders of guilds for every type of craft production from candlesticks to textiles, widowhood took a new dramatic turn in history. The Paris tax list of 1272 shows that there were five exclusively female guilds and that most of the other 120 listed had women members. These were mainly the widows of former guild members. The fact that it was specifically formulated that widows retained the right to train apprentices suggests that these women were as skilled at their trades as their husbands had been. But if the widow re-married she retained her membership only if her new husband was also a member of the same guild, or became one by entering the trade. But if her new husband belonged to another guild she lost the right to train apprentices. This may have been a way of severing her connections with the guild to resolve any dual loyalties incurred by her marriage to a member of another guild, which she might also become entitled to join should he too predecease her.

This was the first time since the order of deaconesses in the 2nd and 3rd centuries that widows were accorded access to specific roles in society by virtue of their status as widows. A tiny proportion of these women even achieved entry into important positions of power and wealth. Four percent of those listed on the prestigious London taxpayers lists of 1319 were women living alone, i.e., mainly wealthy, independent widows.

Medieval widows could attain these positions of prestige and authority in the public sphere because they had not been cut off from society and confined solely to the private domain as wives. In Medieval times, the home was not a private place as it was to become in the Industrial Revolution. It was the site of productivity, the distribution of goods and the accommodation of artisans and apprentices

Widows also enjoyed a special advantage in civil courts since they still had protection under canon law. They were able to appeal to the Church to overrule civil court decisions if these went against them and they used this anomalous situation to further their economic interests as a class. For the first time in history, by gaining some control over their own dowers (inheritance), medieval widows succeeded in making an impact on society. Between 1300 and 1500 'of all medieval women, widows were often the most visible' (Barron & Sutton, 1994). Never again have widows been represented as a class in law nor enjoyed such privileges.

But widows so empowered eventually began to threaten male supremacy in society and the widow gradually became the butt of rumour and ridicule in both the Church and literature. Widows are the perfect target for the projection of fears regarding the loss of male control, as they are indeed released from male control and in medieval literature this anxiety attained new depths. For example, one surviving Medieval story describes how widows would 'cut the head, break the teeth. cut the side, even castrate the body of their dead husbands - if they believed they could better appease their animal-like lust.' In fourteenth century England, Chaucer revived an ancient image of the wanton widow. In the Wife of Bath, described in the Norton Anthology of English Literature as 'the remarkable culmination of centuries of anti-feminism, particularly nurtured by the Medieval Church', Chaucer specifically targets widowhood. Based on the teachings of the fourth century monk, St. Jerome, who blamed women for men's failure to remain celibate, the wife of Bath, widowed four times, is driven by the insatiable lecherousness of her sex to remarry again and again.

In addition, the increasing economic power of widows was also beginning to threaten male supremacy and so, predictably, resistance began to build to the entitlement of widows in the guilds. For example, bakers in France sought to remove widows from their guild in the thirteenth century on the grounds that they weren't strong enough to knead dough. They were overruled by the court and women continued to hold membership in the guilds, albeit under mounting opposition, up until the sixteenth and even seventeenth century in some parts of Europe.

Legally, the medieval widow eventually found herself in an unenviable bind. On the one hand, canon law recommended against remarriage for most widows, widowhood still being viewed by Christianity as a state approaching grace by virtue of its chastity. Civil law codes on the other hand, supported liberalizing the inheritance and remarriage rights of widows. But it was feared that these might encourage women to deceive, or even murder, their husbands in order to marry another man, as divorce was not an option. However, only by remarriage could the widow be put back under male control and her uncontrollable sexuality (and growing economic strength) be reharnessed into legitimate channels. This dilemma may have contributed to the eventual marginalisation of widows from mainstream society altogether.

As long as it lasted, widow-power was an important force in the shaping of medieval Europe. The entry of some widows into spheres not hitherto open to women, endowed *all* widows with special status. And only in widowhood did women have any control over their own lives. No wonder that in medieval times it was sometimes said that 'T'was better to be widowed than married.'

The Reformation

The image of the post-medieval widow deteriorated in tandem with her fortune. The medieval portrayal of the 'merry' widow began to give way to one of a woman sadly alienated from society. During the great religious upheaval of the sixteenth century in central and Western Europe, the Reformed and Protestant churches were split off from Orthodox Catholicism and much original Christian doctrine was revised including that pertaining to marriage and widowhood. The Reformed Church replaced celibacy with marriage as the most desirable state for women, thus eliminating the widow's special spiritual status in religion. *Marriage was henceforth to be the only status in which women could flourish and widows were transformed into the anti-heroine of the now sanctified wife.*

The image of the post-medieval widow began to change from one of empowerment to one of sadness and alienation.

An example of this transformation of the widow into the anti-heroine of her previous self as a wife is to be found in the anonymous Elizabethan poem 'An Olde Woman's Tale in her Solitaire Cell.' The poem relates the experience of a man who, walking deep in the wood, stumbles upon a widow living in her solitary cell in a forest cave. The widow, sulky, pale and melancholic, describes her 20 years as a married woman, flourishing in wealth, beauty and happiness. Her woe, she declares, began when her husband died, leaving her with three children. Now in poverty, forsaken by her husband who did not remember her in his will, in accordance, she claims, with the vile customs of England, she retreats from society to dwell apart, invisible to all but a chance adventurer.

This demotion of the widow persisted through the ensuing centuries right up to the present day. In an essay about widows and spinsters in eighteenth century Britain and France, historian Oliver Hufton wrote, 'any eighteenth-century scholar . . . sees the emergence in literature of *the [single mature woman] as a stereotype . . . one to be despised, pitied and avoided as an eternal spoilsport in the orgy of life'*. Hufton describes women without husbands, whom he calls 'women outside the family' (hors de_la famille), as living in some kind of twilight existence – much as many do still today. Except for the allusion to the 'vile custom' of husbands not providing for their wives in their wills, this allegory could apply unaltered to widowhood today. Many widows several centuries later are still 'retreat(ing) from society to dwell apart', recalling their lives as married women as 'flourishing' and assessing their lives as widows as counting for naught. 'When I was a married woman, I was somebody. Now I am a nobody!' was the way one new widow summed up her new social status in Lynne Caine's account of widowhood several hundred years later. ('Widow' Lynne Caine, 1970)

The Industrial Revolution

The widow's fall from grace, beginning with the decline of the Church's influence during the Renaissance was accelerated by the advent of the Industrial Revolution which began in the second half of the eighteenth century.

. Social attitudes to both motherhood and marriage are socially and economically manipulated phenomena which have changed in status and practice as radically over the centuries as the fashions people wear. Widowhood is the last phase of most married women's lives. It is the successor to marriage and motherhood It should follow logically that the status of widowhood too would also be sensitive to social and economic change. And this has indeed been the case.

The rise of industrialisation began to provide jobs for more and more people, increasing the numbers of those who could now afford to marry. Furthermore, expanding industries needed increasing populations to work in the factories. As a result of these two factors, marriage and motherhood were elevated in the nineteenth century to the highest ideals of womanhood.

Birth rates began to rise and by the 19th century there was an average of six surviving children per family in Victorian England and with child mortality rates as high as 33% for children under age 5, women were averaging around a dozen pregnancies, confining them to the home for most of their married life. The husband became the only link for women to the outside world and his death left the widow socially isolated as well. However, this isolation would probably have been ameliorated by the support of very large families and a very short duration of widowhood (as life expectancies for men and women were about the same).

Modern Widowhood

A major problem for the widows of today is that many were adolescents in the 1950s , wives in the '60s and mothers in the '70s. In the '50s and 60s when these women's images of womanhood were being formed, women's main source of fulfilment was still to be found in marriage and motherhood and most of their efforts were geared to that end. Marriage was the pinnacle of female aspirations and regarded by men and women alike as a privileged position. All people, but especially women who did not marry were considered aberrant and defective in some way. Higher education, for those women who received it, was seldom to achieve a career but rather to equip them to get a more educated husband with higher socio-economic potential. The future husband's status would be conferred by proxy on his wife; she was not expected or encouraged to achieve status through her own efforts. In fact, she was discouraged as working outside the home was considered irresponsible once a woman had children.

For the others, unskilled jobs or trades such as hairdressing, dressmaking, doctor's or dentist's assistants were simply filling in time while finding a husband. Every woman from the wealthiest to the poorest expected to be supported for the rest of her life by her husband. A man, no matter how low his socio-economic class and especially amongst the working class, was ashamed to allow his wife to work for money.

Birth rates fell drastically during the Great Depression (1929 to 1939) and even further During World War II (1939 to 1945) When the soldiers returned to civilian life at the end of World War II, the women who had been keeping the home front going vacated the jobs for returning soldiers and devoted themselves to making up for the deficit of babies who had not been born in the last two decade since the beginning of the Depression .This resulted in largest cohort of any generation in history, labelled the Baby Boomers and the Baby Boomers have now entered the widowhood years . Nearly all women who grew up during these years had full-time mothers (only 10% to 15% of women in the post-World War II years of the fifties had regular paid employment). Most of them became full-time mothers themselves.

In the 1970s, many of these women were exposed to feminist ideas for the first time and, even if their image of marriage as the ideal role of womanhood was challenged, it was usually too late for them to compete with men in the workforce. Women of this transitional generation were thus often unsettled and frustrated by their roles as wife and mother, unlike their own mothers, but unable to change them, unlike their daughters.

In the closing decades of the twentieth century, with the return of women to the workplace, their rising economic independence and the anti-natal stance of most modern governments, due now to the global population explosion the prestige of motherhood withered away leaving only the 'wife' as the most elevated status of women. And if *the wife was now all, then the widow must be nothing, having lost everything.*

Compare this to the situation of widows in early Christian times (see page 30-31), when the wife was nil, soiled by the necessary evil of sex for reproduction and the widow was elevated to a state of grace because of her assumed celibacy. A principle emerges from this comparison: *the status of the widow is inversely related to the status of marriage.*

We are living today in the next great transition of human civilization, from the industrial to the post-industrial world. Widowhood, like everything else, is undergoing rapid and profound changes.

In addition, because women are increasingly outliving men, widowhood has become a longer and increasingly common experience for women than ever before. In previous generations, widows and widowers were more equally matched in number and therefore available to marry one another if they so desired. Furthermore, those who did not choose to remarry would not usually have survived for very long periods as widowed people anyway, as life expectancy was rarely greater than sixty. Single widows and widowers were, therefore, much rarer and friends and relatives could and did, devote time and thought to their needs. But today, as widowhood continues to become more prevalent and prolonged and as society becomes awash with widows, nobody cares any more. *The widowhood experience for this generation of women will be very different from that of their mothers.*

The material welfare of widows and orphans has been a recurrent concern of society, with varying degrees of effectiveness, since the earliest recorded times. From the biblical tithe to the widow's pension, society has endeavoured spasmodically to provide sustenance for widows, while at the same time, except for brief interludes in early Biblical times and in the Middle Ages, depriving them of the possibilities of independence and personhood.

Under the Church's care, widows were protected. But with the declining power of the church, society progressively divested itself of responsibility for widows and their physical plight in recent centuries has, at most times, been terrible – they were burnt as witches in the seventeenth century, reduced to prostitution to feed themselves and their children in the eighteenth century and imprisoned together with their children when they were unable to support them in the nineteenth century.

In the twentieth century, the State finally assumed financial responsibility in most Western countries. Today, in Western societies, with the introduction of the widows pension and full inheritance rights to their husband's estates, few widows face the crucial poverty and deprivations of former centuries, although many still suffer financial loss. But rich or poor, in many respects, widows today still remain second-class citizens.

In the coming years, with the increasing entry of women into the public domain, it is to be hoped that widows will once again find their voice to speak on their own behalf as they are did so briefly long ago in Medieval Europe.

Widowerhood vs. Widowhood

The experience of widowerhood has never been to man, as widowhood is to woman.

As Eve was fashioned out of the rib of Adam, it follows logically that Adam could exist without Eve but Eve could not exist without Adam. Remarkably, the essence of this creation story, that Eve was created out of the body of Adam, still influences the way society views widow- and widower-hood to this day. Consequently, a widower, unlike a widow, is still treated socially as he was before his spouse died. He does not see himself differently and consequently does not lose his sense of self-identity Many women, on the other hand, still adopt their husbands surname: are ranked and rank themselves by their husband's social status and generally identify so profoundly with their husbands that as widows they can often experience an extremely debilitating loss of self-identification.

Loss of status is also a widely reported consequence of widowhood by widows of all economic classes. It is not only a social reaction to widows but many widows themselves report feeling a loss of self- worth on becoming a widow. But no such loss of status or feelings of worthlessness assail the widower. In fact, his status and popularity are more likely to be raised because they are a commodity in short supply and great demand. Today, over the age of 65 there are around five times the number of widows to widowers in most advanced first world country. This numerical distortion is responsible for many of the profound differences in societies treatment of widows and widowers.

Furthermore, widowers, unlike widows, are not burdened with the legacy of being seen as a threat to the social order, as ascribed throughout the ages to sexually mature females not under the control of a husband or the Church. Because the widower is not seen as a threat, he does not have to endure society's marginalisation, stereotyping, denial or discrimination reserved only for widows. The widower actually gains more sexual freedom by virtue of his widowerhood.

Throughout history widows have been discouraged from re-marrying because it was regarded, among other reasons, as a dis-loyalty to her dead spouse. Widowers on the other hand, can re-marry, start dating (and even multiple date) as soon as they wish after their wives die not only with social approval but encourage-ment. And the women they marry will be usually a generation younger than themselves Part of this irrational difference in atti-tude to widowers in contrast to widows has probably derived from the legacy of ancient practices. It would have been advantageous to the human species for older widowers to marry younger women, because anatomically men could go on fathering children to the end of their lives whereas women could only reproduce up to the menopause, which is believed to have been considerably earlier in ancient times (Aristotle refers to menopause at age 40 compared to average age of 51 for menopause to-day). But undoubtedly a major reason for the different social attitude to widows and wid-owers has been the excess of widows and paucity of widowers at every stage in history because widowers have usually been en-couraged in most cultures to remarry. while widows have not.

Even though the widowerhood experience appears to be so much easier for widowers than widowhood is for widows, para-doxically, mortality rates for widowers in the first two years after the death of their wives are higher than for married men of the same age , while mortality rates for widows do not differ from those of still married women . Obviously, the successful adjust-ment to widowhood and widowerhood is a complex process which cannot be achieved simply by replacing the lost spouse.

CHAPTER 3

Till death do us part

Marriage as the precursor of widowhood.

A major purpose of marriage is to promote the success of child survival. In pre-modern times marriage, childbearing and childrearing spanned most of a woman's adult life, from the menarche to menopause, which occurred only a few years before death. Widowhood, on the other hand, lasted only for a short period, as men and women lived approximately the same length of time. But since the latter part of the twentieth century, the child rearing phase and the widowhood phase quite often each endure for about twenty years. If child rearing is valued as a positive gain of marriage and widowhood as a negative cost of marriage, it follows that, whilst in pre-modern times the benefits of marriage far outweighed the cost, in modern times this is no longer the case. This drastic shift in the benefit/cost ratio is now, among other things, causing sweeping changes to the traditional form of marriage.

Prior to the Industrial revolution, marriage in the Western world was primarily an economic contract for the purpose of having children (Cherfas & Gribbin, 1983). It should be noted that there is an ambiguity in knowing whether marriages were formal or simply pair-bonds in any discussion of marriage and widowhood prior to the twentieth century. Formal marriage in Ancient

Rome, for example, was only permitted by law for upper classes, mainly patrician families. Slaves were forbidden to marry, but nevertheless pair-bonding and partner loss were normal life experiences.

While not forbidden in subsequent eras, marriage was not available to the masses due to economic rather than legal restrictions. In feudal societies it was usual for only the oldest son in a family to marry because he alone would inherit land. In the early nineteenth century, 60-65 per cent of adult women were singles who had never married. Today, this figure is less than 30 per cent and less than 6 per cent for women aged 40 years or more. That is, by age 40, more than 94 per cent of women in Western societies have married at least once.

Romantic love and sexual fulfilment before the nineteenth century were not part of marriage in Judeo-Christian tradition. The Ketubah, the ancient Hebrew marriage contract, does not mention the word love (though in contrast to Christian doctrine, which regarded sex, even in marriage, as an unfortunate necessity for reproduction and not be enjoyed, Jewish men were instructed to gratify their wives sexually). In Renaissance Europe, it was acceptable for men to find sexual excitement and gratification outside marriage with prostitutes and in adulterous liaisons. Sex in marriage was for reproduction. Sex for pleasure was only for men and to be found outside marriage. This was the accepted way of life. Women, for their part, did not look for emotional involvement with their husbands - but rather for support for the family and marriages were arranged with little or no regard for either party's personal preferences in a partner.

Up until the twentieth century, when communal wealth rose enormously, less than 50 per cent of the population in Western countries ever married and marriage was in itself a sign of affluence. A man had to be wealthy enough to support a wife and family to marry.

Similarly, in polygamous societies the wealthier a man, the more wives he could afford. The very wealthiest had the most, with sheikhs and kings (like Solomon) having as many as a thousand. Even today, the West African pop idol, Mongo Faya, has eighty wives (Morris, 1997). But the norm has usually been between two to four.

Only with the advent of the Industrial Revolution did economic conditions improve sufficiently for the masses to begin to devote time to matters other than physical survival. Sexual and emotional preferences then began to enter into the choice of marriage partners. Romantic love, rather than economic advantage, began to be promoted as the new basis for marriage. This shift was itself economically driven to encourage universal marriage in the service of rapidly industrialising societies that needed expanding populations to man their burgeoning factories.

In pre-modern times, without efficient birth control, most married women were either pregnant or lactating for most of their fertile years. With infant death rates over 50 per cent, families ended up with relatively few surviving children. With the increasing wealth created by the Industrial Revolution, infant death rates fell and with the increased proportion of the population marrying as well, populations rapidly expanded.

Advances in technology have progressively released people from the necessity to toil exclusively for survival, increasing time and energy available for other activities. This allowed a fundamental change in attitudes towards marriage as the wealth of industrialising societies increased. With this rising communal wealth and as more and more people could afford it, marriage became progressively more achievable with 75-80 per cent of people marrying by the beginning of the twentieth century and 95 per cent by its end.

Romantic love eventually replaced economic considerations as the conventional reason to marry. Whereas previously people did not expect much emotional or sexual fulfilment from marriage, now these factors became paramount. It is only since the Industrial Revolution that everyone has expected to marry and only those who were born since then that have assumed that marriages are made in heaven. In our times, the expectation of psychological and sexual fulfilment in marriage has become the very essence of marriage itself.

For the last two hundred years the universalisation of marriage based on romance, rather than affordability, has served its primary purpose well - to increase birth rates. And, not surprisingly, *marriage was elevated to the ultimate goal and fulfilment of womanhood.*

The marriage vows are still taken by most people 'till death do us part' with the expectation that emotional and sexual fulfilment in marriage will endure until the end. That this is not so is well attested by divorce rates rising to around 50 per cent in the second half of the twentieth century when most restrictions on divorce, both legal and social, had finally disappeared.

Now in the post-industrial era this idealised nineteenth century version of marriage is cracking under the pressure of over-populated aging societies. Romantic coupling, devised to promote the universalisation of marriage to facilitate rapid growth of population needed by industrialising societies, cannot possibly continue to serve the interests of post-industrial societies which now need to curb population growth.

We obviously need to reassess the purpose and style of marriage to suit the century ahead of us. Childrearing is now completed by parents in middle age instead of, as previously, near the end of their lives. After our children have grown up and left home, women should be cultivating lifestyles more independent of their spouses, instead of the reverse as now occurs, in view of the inevitable extended years of widowhood ahead.

Women with retired husbands often feel restricted from socialising alone even during the daytime as the husband will be left
alone. And, as he nears the end of his life, often as much as twenty
years ahead of her, she is very likely to find herself more and more
confined to the home in the years immediately preceding widowhood. The new widow suddenly finds that her universe once filled
by one man is now empty and meaningless and she is cut adrift
without a place in it.

Marriage since the twentieth century has disadvantaged many
women causing them loneliness, depression, loss of autonomy,
loss of identity and ultimately, in widowhood, loss of self-identification.

The facts support this draconian indictment. Women exhibit no
increase in psychiatric disorders characterised by anxiety and depression as they age as long as they do not marry. Single women
over 35 do not differ in this respect from single women in their
early twenties. Only amongst married women do anxiety disorders
increase with age (Gottman, 1994).

Jessica Bernard, (Future of Marriage, 1972) from her admit-
tedly women's liberationist view states that women are increasingly finding the cost of marriage too high. She then proceeds to
enumerate the costs as loss of independence, freedom and adventure, but as usual, ne'er a mention of widowhood. Yet, it was my
encounter with widowhood that first prompted me to question the
wisdom of marriage as it has survived into the twenty first century.

"Marriage in its present form is an institution that primarily
benefits men", reports University of Washington psychologist,
Neil Jacobson (USA Today, 1993). "As we close the twentieth
century, we are increasingly seeing women distressed in marriage"
(Sheehy, 1995) and, I would add, in its aftermath - widowhood.

The romanticisation of marriage

At the beginning of the 20th century the chances of either a husband or wife surviving the other was unpredictable. But women
today know that the odds are four to one that they will outlive their
spouses. By contrast, at the beginning of the century, parents with
an average number of children faced a 62 per cent chance of losing
a young child. By the late 1970s, this probability had dropped to 4
per cent. *The loss of a child has ceased to be a normal anticipated
part of family life whereas the loss of a husband has become one.*

In former times, it was not only the lives of children but also
life expectancies in general which were far less predictable. People
could expect to lose parents, siblings and children randomly at all
phases of family life.

Because of this, historians and sociologists have suggested
that, in the past, people were reluctant to form strong attachments
to family members. Loyalty and devotion were directed to the
family as a group and even to the clan (Skolnick, 1978).

With the increasing expectation that children would outlive
their parents, emotional attachment to them became safer. Today,
because the death of a child is rare and unexpected it is therefore
far more traumatic to parents than in the past. And yet the loss of
a husband, which is today an 80 per cent probability and, therefore,
a common and normal experience, *is now rated as the most traumatic event to befall a woman in the post-industrial world.*
(Holmes and Rahe, 1967)

Alvin Toffler predicted that in a future of increasing mobility
and fleeting relationships we will again 'learn to avoid total commitment to guard against the pain of disaffiliation' (Toffler, 1970).
This may already be evident in young people's increasing wari-
ness of commitment to marriage in view of the high divorce rate,
a substantial proportion of them having themselves come from
broken homes. But despite the extended years of widowhood,

women have shown little inclination as yet to protect themselves against the pain of losing a husband.

Grief over the loss of a child or a spouse has always been a universal human experience. However, the intensity of that grief varies from culture to culture and with changing times and customs.

.Forearmed with the knowledge that 90 per cent of women who marry will have to face either divorce or widowhood, it may be wiser for modern women to emulate the attitude to children of pre-nineteenth century parents' and not to invest too much emotion in a single partner. It may be better for them to spread their coin further in a number of close Platonic relationships with both sexes

The romanticisation of the lost spouse

No matter whether the husband was a good or bad spouse, many widows romanticise the memory of their deceased husbands. It is akin to a new romantic passion which this time round will form the basis of a posthumous marriage. It is not uncommon to hear widows speaking of their dead husbands, even those who were bad husbands, as though they were back in the first bloom of pre-marital romantic love. The deceased husband can become as idealised and unreal as the first love of a besotted teenager.

Romanticising the memory of the deceased husband appears to be a re-enactment of the romanticisation of marriage. The process is not difficult to visualise. Once the husband dies, the mundane difficulties of everyday life with him will soon recede from memory. Thus, in a program on women who do not enjoy sex with their husbands, Oprah Winfrey found that 40 000 000 married women in the USA were suffering from reduced libido after the birth of their first child and that their desire for less sex in their marriages was causing considerable marital friction. Once a husband dies, these wives will, in general, cross from a situation of too much sexual demand on them to too little. They will soon re-press the memory of a sexually taxing relationship and replace it with a passionate longing for the loss of a sexual partner. Simi-larly, the annoyances of a domineering husband who demanded his favourite food, that he drive the car whenever he was there to do so, that they turn out the light when he wanted to go to sleep – in other words, all the annoying minutiae of co-habitation - will very soon recede. Instead, the loneliness, the lack of intimacy, the lack of support, of shared grief and shared happiness will loom large in their place. It would be difficult indeed to retain a realistic image of the lost partner. Long after romantic love has evaporated in marriage, it seems to be reconstitutable in widowhood and to serve precisely the same purpose – now to hold the widow faithful, no longer to the man, but to his memory. Furthermore, it is the widow herself who is invoking the technique of romantic idealisa-tion to hold herself captive in a marriage which no longer exists.

This somewhat speculative reasoning is necessary to explain the extraordinary phenomenon of widows idealising even the most horrific of marriages. Again and again when speaking with wid-ows I have been struck by the rose-coloured spectacles through which they recall their deceased husbands. I find that most widows see their loss as exceptional and therefore more than every other widow's. Trying to tell new widows in deep grief that time does help is usually counter-productive because of this idealisation. 'it won't help me because this was different', is the response I have come to expect. In other words, 'it may have helped you because your loss wasn't as great as mine'.

This unrealistic idealisation of the deceased spouse, whether following a good or bad marriage, is destructive to the widow. It fosters the suppression of all that was wrong or even simply ordi-nary about her former life. This leads her quickly to the illusion that everything in that former life when she had a husband was good and sweet and wonderful and everything in her new life without him is bad and miserable and hopeless. From this perception of her life, it is only one short step to the conviction that she cannot be a person in her own right, that without a husband she cannot make a new life for herself, cannot stand on her own two feet and that widowhood will be just a matter of sitting it out to the end.

The case against monogamy

If monogamy is now exacting such a heavy price from women as it appears to be (elevated depression and anxiety-related illnesses, up to 50 per cent divorce rates; 80 per cent of women who remain married being widowed for periods extending for decades), one may be forgiven for wondering why most Australian women still marry and many more co-habit without formally marrying. (Australian Census 2012). One reason is undoubtably still to have children. Figures are not available concerning the numbers of de facto couples that marry in order to have children, or legitimise existing children, but the steep rise in single parent families (over half a million in Australia today) indicates that this is a declining motive for marrying today. The only remaining motive appears to be social pressure. There is the lingering view in our society that for a mature woman 'single is bad, married is good' Despite the steep rise in divorce rates since the 1970s, today more married women, compared to unmarried women, rate themselves as happy. This apparent paradox is the result of the indoctrination of girls from early adolescence which leads them to believe that marriage is the sine qua non for happiness. One of the prerequisites for happiness is to escape being 'an old maid'. Forty-one per cent of married women cite one of their reasons for marriage was to escape the disrespect of society for single women (Hite, 1987). *If marriage is a prerequisite for happiness, it then follows that once widowed, one must be unhappy.*

The majority of older women alive today have grown up in societies which expect people to marry. Most have never known any other way of visualising their lives. And not to marry is still an aberration in our culture. This leads to the bizarre situation of over 90 per cent of the population continuing to marry, even though 50 per cent will eventually divorce and unknown numbers will stay in dysfunctional, even violent marriages to avoid the stigma, not anymore of divorce, but singleness.

Thinking back now to my own childhood and adolescence, I recall how I used to fantasise about the boy somewhere growing up, going to school, playing on the beaches of Sydney, who would one day be my husband. The thought never crossed my mind, never once, that I might not marry at all in the end. That boy existed somewhere as surely as the sun would rise the next morning.

Twenty years later, in the sixties, after I was divorced and living with another man, my aged father said to him, 'I want my daughter to be happy and I approve of anything you do to make her so. But I ask only one thing of you - I want to see her a married woman again before I die'. Even though my father was born in 1896, he was able to accept my adultery but not my loss of marital status, because by now only singleness, but not divorce or adultery, engendered lack of respectability and rejection by society. Remarkably, I did not see his request as in any way unreasonable or extraordinary.

And two decades later, 56 per cent of married women were still citing social acceptability as a major reason for having married and among the reasons given by women for staying married, more stated that social acceptability is a more relevant factor than economic security or intimacy (Hite, 1987). ***Marriage as an institution in Western society may be breaking down, but singleness remains an uncomfortable alternative for women.***

Defacto, polygynous and serial marriages

Because of the huge excess of divorced and widowed women, serial marriages, de facto and polygynous arrangements are increasing - the former openly, the latter still clandestinely. If the shortage of males available for marriage continues to increase or even maintain present levels, it can be expected that polygynous unions will increase and finally come 'out of the closet' with second wives seeking legal recognition. It is interesting to note that already thirty years ago, in a study on retirement marriage by W. C. McKain, it was suggested that polygamy for men and women past the age of sixty be legalised (Hafner, 1993). An excess of 4.5 million females over age 65 was being predicted in the middle of the century to be reached before 1985 in the United States. By 1999, the excess had in fact exceeded 10 million and still today no such law has been enacted or even mooted. But reality may have overtaken planning. De facto polygamous marriages are probably more prevalent than is commonly imagined. That they are now becoming socially acceptable was demonstrated by the world-wide telecasting of the de facto wife and her illegitimate daughter alongside the legal wife and children at the state funeral of the President of France, President Mitterand.

For one of her chat shows televised early in 1999, Oprah Winfrey invited women who had discovered that their husbands had other wives to write to her. Amongst the copious replies was an account of a man's funeral at which so many putative wives turned up that none of them knew who was the legal wife.

Due to the dramatic rise in life expectancies and in divorce rates throughout the Western world, second and even third marriages are becoming common. This trend is giving rise to yet another form of marriage today called 'serial marriage'.

These changes which are challenging the old concepts of exclusivity and permanence in marriage will inevitably profoundly affect the future experience of widowhood.

But that future is difficult to predict. As modern medicine is advancing, the difference in benefit between men and women is lessening. As a result, the excess of women to men aged 65 and over in the U.S. has receded from 10 million in 1999 to 6 million in 2019, despite an increase of 50 million in the total population. It is interesting to compare the attitudes to remarriage of widows of the most technologically advanced societies in the world with that of the most primal - the Australian Aborigines (Lawler, 1991). Aboriginal girls are married off at the time of their first menstruation in tribally arranged marriages. Men are not permitted to marry until they are much older - usually between 26 and 40 years of age. They must first undergo a protracted period of personal and spiritual development in order to earn the right to a wife. Men are allowed as many wives as they like, as long as they are skilled enough and strong enough to fulfil their marital obligations, ie., there is a polygynous system for men. Women, on the other hand, can have only one husband at a time, but from first menstruation to death they are never without a husband, ie., they are allowed serial monogamous marriages.

Women move immediately from one husband to the next when their much older spouses die as polygyny ensures no shortage of available partners.

As women grow older, the age pattern for marriage reverses. Older, sexually experienced widows are betrothed to newly initiated young men marrying for the first time. Very old widows, who may not any longer be able to find willing partners, are provided for matrimonially by the kinship system which requires a man to marry his older brother's widow, no matter how old she is. (Compare this with the practice of Levirate marriage of the Jews whereby a man is only required to marry his brother's widow if she is childless, not to protect her, but to ensure that his brother's genes survive into the future by impregnating her!)

Women are considered and consider themselves, to be sexually attractive into advanced old age and sexual attraction is a consideration in the remarriage of widows. Compare this with the loss of status and ambiguous sexuality of the modern Western widow. When entering subsequent marriages, widows are given freedom of choice in contrast to the first marriage which is tribally arranged purely with a view to childbearing.

Individual sexual desire is also fulfilled through extramarital relationships which are socially acceptable and common, especially for women, as men have more than one wife anyhow. During the long years of preparation, it is considered prestigious for younger unmarried men to have several liaisons with older women, all of whom are of course married as there are no unmarried adult females.

Consequently, in Aboriginal society, there are no spinsters, no old maids, no maiden aunts, no widows and very few divorced people. Divorce is allowed but hardly ever needed in such a caring and individually satisfying marriage system. And women, like men in our society, are not diminished sexually by advancing age. In the search for new models of female-male relationships, the post-modern Western world could profit from a closer look at a society like this one in which marriage has evolved primarily to serve its members, instead of the religious, demographic, technological and economic demands of successive ages.

The marital status of widowhood - wives without husbands

Widows are often confused about their new marital status. Officially, they are single again but nonetheless they are still seen as attached to their dead husbands. They ***remain wives without husbands.***

This is the legacy of thousands of years in which wives were considered to be the property of their husbands. Widows were part of a deceased man's estate. In some cultures they were burnt or buried with him. In others, they were inherited along with the children and other goods and chattels of the estate by the male next of kin.

Today they remain ambiguously attached to their deceased husbands and former status of married woman. Widows are still accorded the title of 'Mrs' in Western countries and, so I have found that I am still addressed as Mrs. Wolfers by anyone who does not feel comfortable with me on first-name terms. But the title does not sit easily with me anymore. I am ambivalent about it because on the one hand, I feel fraudulent if the person addressing me doesn't know that I am widowed (and this will usually be the case with anyone not on first-name terms with me); on the other hand, I am reluctant to reveal that I am widowed because it should be irrelevant, but in reality I find that people react to me differently once they know I am widowed. Perhaps I still wear my wedding ring for this reason or perhaps to avoid being seen as a single person. But in any event, I feel it would be a disloyalty to my husband to remove it, which I know is ridiculous.

As it is, I still feel myself to be a married woman. In the persisting perception of Western society that 'married' is better than 'not married', that attachment to a male is necessary for female fulfilment, that married women are somehow more wholesome and legitimate than unmarried ones, this remains a more comfortable image for me to live with.

Adultery

With the increasing availability of unattached women it is highly probable that adultery on the part of married men with widowed and divorced females is increasing.

When I was first widowed I thought that I had lost my eligibility to flirt with married men. I felt that as I no longer had a husband to offer even in the innocent sexual tension games that married couples often play, I was no longer in an equal playing field with married women. When I was a married woman I did not feel restrained from socially acceptable flirtations with other women's husbands. But once widowed I saw myself coming to the party as a pauper, empty-handed and asking for a hand-out.

But as time has passed and I have become more aware of the sexual realities of widowhood, I have come to see the situation of widows in adulterous relations quite differently - almost a total turnabout.

In the nineteenth century, the Darwinian-Westermarck thesis explained the survival of monogamy as the result of male need for fidelity of his female (but not of himself) to be sure of his paternity. This thinking was reversed by the twentieth century sociologist Kingsley Davis who claimed that it was not male jealousy that gave rise to monogamy but monogamy that gave rise to jealousy.

Whatever the theory, surveys have convincingly demonstrated that men aspire to multi-sexual encounters for themselves far more than do women. One survey found that twice as many husbands (41 per cent) as wives (22 per cent) expressed an interest in mate-swapping (Psychology Today, July,1970). Traditionally, extra-marital sex has been tolerated for men but not women (Morton, 1997). Up until the twentieth century, sex within marriage was for the purpose of bearing children; sex for pleasure was to be sought in brothels or adulterous affairs for which, if discovered, only the female was seriously censured. *The sexual double standards of the nineteenth century still apply to widowhood in the twenty-first century.*

Thus, it is more acceptable for a widower to remarry soon after the death of his spouse than for a widow. Widowers can date as many women as they please without incurring social censure but a widow in a relationship with even two men simultaneously is viewed as promiscuous.

Today, with the extended years of life, there is more time than ever before for marriages to become stale. With the huge excess of women over men, who are either widowed or divorced we may expect a resurgence of this Victorian view of sex for pleasure outside of marriage. As long as husbands honour their legal obligations to their wives, a little fun on the side may again be the order of the day.

Infidelity with a widow does not involve men in betraying other women's husbands, often their own friends, but only their own wives. And this appears preferable to many. Perhaps there is also an element of graciousness in caring for the widow of a deceased friend.

Lynne Caine offers yet another explanation. 'The worst part is' she writes, 'that wives are often right. A widow is like Mt. Everest to most men. They seem to have to make her, just because she's there.' (Caine L.1974)

Whatever the explanation, I have little doubt now that widows do fulfil a sexual role in the extending years of marriage and that the traditional fears of wives of this role is not entirely unjustified. But given the demographic pressure of our times, wives may even prefer to become as tolerant of their husbands' peccadilloes as they were in former times rather than risk being 'dumped for younger wives and second lives'(See chapter 5)

Remarriage

Remarriage of widows was not discouraged in ancient Israel. Nonetheless, because the Hebrew Bible pays so much attention to the care of widows, it would appear that there were many widows who did not remarry. Perhaps there was a shortage of men due to their frequent battles with the pagan world.

The Christian religion by contrast, discouraged remarriage of widows. The idea of sex for any reason other than procreation was a sin and so the concept of remarriage for older women came into conflict with Christian ideology. But also in pagan society sexual abstinence by widows seems to have been socially demanded. Ovid referred to widows who did not behave chastely as 'wanton old hags', a shame to society.

The early Church was particularly adamant in its views concerning the chastity of widowhood. It exhorted all widows not to remarry and to remain faithful to their dead husbands for the rest of their lives. In Rome in 354 AD the Emperor Constantius forbade the abduction of virgins and widows for the purpose of marrying them. Then in 380 the Emperor Theodesius issued an edict prohibiting the forcing of widows to remarry.

Things were obviously very different from today. When there was not a surplus of women, widows were in demand as marriage partners. Furthermore, it appears that widows themselves may not all have been so eager to remarry. Jerome, a renowned Christian scholar of the fourth century explained that, 'because they have experienced the authority of their husbands, they prefer the license of widowhood' (Ep. 22:16). *Not all widows at all times have regarded widowhood as the unmitigated disaster that many do today.*

By contrast, widowers appear always to have been free to remarry with society's help and approval. Even in times when there were more men than women, widowers remarried at higher rates than widows (See Appendix *, Table 2).

Ironically, only now in the 21st century when it is virtually impossible for most widows to find a new partner has it become culturally desirable for them to do so. How many times have I been told by well-meaning friends to 'get myself a man'. Not only is it now socially acceptable for a widow to enter into a new intimate relationship with or without formally marrying, but society often penalises those who don't.

50 years ago, before the dramatic rise in divorce rates, widows had far more opportunity to remarry than they do today. In 1971, 23 per cent of women involved in a marriage where one partner was remarrying were widows, while 45 per cent were divorcees. The increase in divorced women looking for second husbands has squeezed an already scarce market even harder. Remarriage for the majority of widows is now a very remote option. The statistics today reveal a very grim situation for widows, especially older widows, who set their sights on finding a new male partner. Not only are there four times as many widows as there are widowers, but the majority of the 20 per cent of married men who do outlive their wives will remarry women far younger than the majority of that 80 per cent of women who outlive their husbands. Widowers over the age of sixty-five are more likely today to seek new wives amongst the surplus of available younger divorced women. (There are today in the United States over 3,000,000 million and in Australia, over 100 000, more divorced women than divorced men. This excess of divorced women is due to the fact that divorced men are re-marrying at a much higher rate than divorced women.)

In addition, the excess of unattached, widows and divorcees will be further exacerbated by a new social pattern which is currently emerging of men rejecting marriage altogether. In a women's journal article entitled 'Men Who'll Never Marry', the following cross section of answers given by several of the interviewees illustrates the social consequences of an excess of females and job insecurity for males.

Tony, fitness instructor, aged 22.

'There are too many women in the world to ever consider the prospect of marriage. I'm having a great time (just) sampling what's out there . . .'

Paul, masseur, aged 40

'I've been with my partner 15 years . . . . Now I can't see any point in getting married'.

Adam, political researcher, aged 34

It worries Adam that he's never lived with a woman and he fears that he may not be able to 'make somebody happy'. But the sexual freedom is addictive; 'I know men who show no sign of ever giving that up: it's like a drug'.

John, journalist, aged 36

'My family experience shows marriage doesn't necessarily work'. He fears the financial trap of a formalised commitment.

Tom, engineer, aged 36

'My dad had four kids and a steady job – I can't even be sure of supporting myself today'.

In the USA there are 5 million and in Australia over half a million, more never-married men than women. The majority of this excess is, in both cultures, under 35 years of age. This reluctance of younger men to commit themselves can be expected to increase the availability of younger women to older divorced and widowed men, thus further depleting the pool of available partners for widows, especially older ones.

In previous generations when the excess of widows over widowers was smaller and widowhood itself was a shorter experience, both widows and widowers must have commonly entered widowhood with the expectation of remarrying - at least with the expectation that the option would be there if they chose to pursue it.

Today this is no longer true. Most widows soon come to the conclusion that remarriage, or a stable new partnership, is so remote a possibility that it is not worth pursuing. Helena Lopata in one of the few studies to date on widows' attitudes found that 'few widows expect that they will be able to find another husband' (1987). Comments commonly heard amongst widows on this subject are:

'There is no-one out there anymore'

'If there is an available man, the odds are there is something wrong with him or he'd have been snapped up already.'

'Even if you do find a suitable man at seventy, the odds are there will soon be something wrong with him.'

There is a point of strain in demographic disparities which, if exceeded, leads to total collapse. This is the situation of the marriage market for widows today. The shortage of available men has become so acute that the usual rules of supply and demand have broken down. Widows are fast approaching the view that remarriage is no longer a viable option in widowhood. The dyadic strength (due to scarcity) of men in this population is now so great that most can successfully compete for women in younger groups of surplus females. And those that can't will probably not be worth the candle. There are of course successful and rewarding recouplings in widowhood. But these are exceptional and should not be held up as paradigms for widows to emulate. They are winners in a lottery with very poor odds.

Only about one in ten widows over the age of sixty will re-marry. And for this 10 per cent, remarriage will be a hazardous undertaking. The age gap between men and women involving a second marriage for one or both partners can be expected to keep increasing the greater the imbalance between available men and women becomes. The odds are that younger widows who remarry much older men will soon face widowhood again. And there is an even greater hazard now emerging as a truly terrifying prospect for women who marry 'old' men. Because modern medical ad-vances enable terminally ill people to be kept alive for much longer periods than in former times, more and more women are becoming long-term carers for ailing husbands.

When weighed in the balance, the disadvantages of remarrying appear to outweigh the advantages except in one area - that of so-cial conformity in our couple based societies. And this remains a major reason for marriage at any age.

Nevertheless, just as with marriage, fashions in the cultural at-titudes to singledom are also changing. In times past, when in-crease in the population was economically desirable, as after heavy death tolls from war or disease or in times of increasing prosperity as in the Industrial Revolution, there was increased so-cial pressure on people to marry. At these times, bachelors and 'old maids' were stigmatised. This was a means for accelerating population growth. ***But today there is a need to reduce the popu-lation and, still, society penalises singledom.***

However conventional marriage, still the norm in all Western societies, is now starting to crumble. In her book "The Improvised Woman", the novelist Marcelle Clements challenges the old con-cepts:

'Spinster, old maid, maiden aunt – the single woman has never had a good press The single woman's state has long been regarded as a misfortune or a threat'. But Clements claims that today the word 'single' is too narrow. These days, 'single' covers women who, by choice, have never married, serial cohabitees between relationships, women who take lovers but prefer to live alone, mothers who choose single parenthood as well as divorcees and widows. 'Single' certainly is no longer synonymous with celibate or desperate. Nor is 'single' or 'married' any longer a fixed state, but rather a description of a woman's current status which is very much open to change.

'Delayed marriage, divorce rates, low marriage rates and longer life-spans have created a world in which most women can expect to be married for only half of their adult lives', (M Clements. 1999)

These new social statistics are challenging marriage as the norm of social organisation in the Western world. To date, one cannot refer to adult relationships by any other term than 'marital status'. It is the generic term encompassing single, divorced, separated, widowed and married on all legal documents and government censuses. And the married state is the baseline from which all other categories are defined.

A single person is a person who is not married.

A separatee is a person who has married and is now living apart from his or her spouse.

A divorcee is a person who was married and no longer is.

A widow is a person who was married but whose partner has died.

A person in a de facto relationship is defined as one living with a partner but not married to him or her.

But it is becoming apparent that we are at a turning point in the public perception of the status of marriage. While 'it is still true that very few of my female contemporaries would have made staying single their first choice . . . at the very least it has become an option that seems preferable to some others and at most it is an opportunity for a life that is, in a number of ways, richer', writes Clements.

Viewing singledom as a choice, 60 years ago was confined to the extremists of the Women's Liberation Movement. Today, it has become acceptable that many women will not settle for marriage at any price or for marriage with the best available if the best available is not good enough but choose instead to endure the social penalty for remaining single.

And it is important to singles of *all* varieties that singledom is becoming a status of choice for *some people* , because where there is choice there is dignity and respect. Whether we are discussing where widows live, or celibacy or singledom, the option to choose is a prime determinant of status for the individuals involved. Even if only some individuals in a group can exercise choice, the status of the whole group benefits. Female singles, as a class, can no longer *all* be labelled as spinsters, old maids and maiden aunts since there are amongst them now those who *choose* to be single. And, conversely, marriage can no longer be the most important goal of every maiden's dreams since there are some amongst them now some who *choose* to reject it.

A 1997 study entitled "Family Values in the Nineties", in which the Australian Institute for Family Studies surveyed 9000 women, found a marked difference in attitudes to marriage between women under thirty and those over thirty. The younger women were more accepting of single parenting, homosexuality, homosexual parents, people never marrying and de facto marriage. But as Dr David de Vaus, the author of this report, pointed out, it was as yet not possible to say whether the women in their twenties, in this survey were in fact in the vanguard of a change in traditional attitudes or whether their views would become more traditional as they themselves grew older.

Marriage is the progenitor of widowhood. At the beginning of the 21st century, traditional marriage is undergoing profound changes which will inevitably affect the experience of widowhood. Whom, how and for how long, (and even if) , we marry are progressively becoming less a matter of law and more a matter of choice. As traditional heterosexual permanent marriage gives way to de facto, serial, polygamous and sexually amorphous arrangements and as the boundaries between singles and couples and between sexually active and celibate people recede, it is predictable that many of the present negative experiences still challenging, widows today will also fade.

CHAPTER 4

The deepest cut of all

It is widely accepted that the death of a spouse is the single most impactful change that can befall a person, ie., the one causing the most change in the shortest time (Toffler, 1970).

Toffler defined future shock as 'the human response to over-stimulation'. Its symptoms range from anxiety, hostility and violence to physical illness, depression and apathy. Its victims often manifest erratic swings in interest and lifestyle, followed by social, intellectual and emotional withdrawal. They feel 'continually bugged and harassed and want desperately to reduce the number of decisions they must make'.

This syndrome accurately describes my initial reactions to widowhood. During the first months after my husband died I was psychologically paralysed. I would go to the supermarket and return with nothing, unable to decide what I needed. My first major chore was to find an apartment to use as an office. I found it difficult even to select which ones to inspect from the real estate agent's lists and once selected, I could not decide what would be suitable. In the end, my daughter had to lease an apartment for me.

It is not surprising that the symptoms resulting from over-stimulation and spousal bereavement are similar. The loss of a spouse usually ends the longest and most intimate of all human relationships. It affects every moment and every aspect of one's life. It will result in greater change to the surviving spouse's life than any other normal human experience. If a child dies, the grief may be unbearable, but the parents will still go to bed together, rise together the next day, hang their towels side-by-side in the bathroom, confide in each other and eventually return to their normal lives together, no matter with how much sadness in their hearts. But the loss of a spouse, even following a bad marriage, cuts into every minute of one's existence, often with the suddenness of a guillotine.

During the late sixties, two psychiatrists, Holmes and Rahe, designed the Life-Change Unit Scale (LCUS), intended to measure how much change a person has experienced in a given span of time. This effect they named the *impactfulness* of an event. They found in their research that the death of a spouse was rated by the majority of people as the most traumatic or impactful event in a normal human life. Accordingly, they assigned it a score of 100 points on the LCUS. Moreover, when this scale was rated by widely differing populations in countries widely separated around the world, the order for severity of stress for the different items remained remarkably constant. Death of a spouse appears to be the most stressful event for both men and women in most cultures.

Using this instrument, Holmes and Rahe demonstrated that there was a strong correlation between one's score on the LCUS and risk of illness in the following year. Those people who had high scores were most likely to fall ill and, furthermore, the higher the score the more severe the illness was likely to be.

A series of British studies have strongly suggested that the onset of widowhood weakens resistance to illness leading to increased pathology and mortality for the surviving spouse (Carnegie Trust, 1993). In past generations when the average duration of widowhood was comparatively short, this would not have been so significant. But today, with a potential duration of widow-

hood approaching twenty years, it is important to address this phenomenon and counsel newly widowed women in the management
of the psychological and physical effects of bereavement.

It is now widely accepted that excessive anxiety and depression
in grief can lead to pathology. For example Takotsubo a sudden
and acute form of heart failure, (also called broken heart syndrome) can occur as a direct consequence of excessive grief . .
However, it is now thought that it may not be only grief that causes
pathology in widowhood but also the high impact that loss of a
spouse incurs, forcing the survivor to make a multitude of major
life changes within a short period. It seems that an enormous number of changes within a short period may overwhelm the body's
coping mechanisms.

It would appear prudent therefore that avoidable changes
should, as far as possible, be kept to a minimum, for at least the
first year of widowhood e .g. change of job, changes of domicile,
acquisition of new relationships, removal from old friends, familiar places of work, shopping, entertainment. Although a widow
must eventually find a new life and a new identity, the medical
indications appear to be that this cannot be undertaken too quickly,
that time is needed to allow adaptation to the impact of the enormous and pervasive changes occasioned by widowhood. Yet widows are still being encouraged by professionals and friends alike
to actively seek out a new life for themselves as quickly as possible. I recall how painful and futile were my own early attempts to
please friends and relatives by co-operating with such well-meaning efforts of friends to introduce me to new people. And I forced
myself to look for new activities, like joining adult education classes, taking a trip abroad, co-operating in a blind date arranged by
mutual friends, going to a wedding alone a month after David died
and so on. Some of these activities were extremely painful, but I
regarded them as necessary to my adjustment to life without David. I treated them like a new ill-fitting pair of shoes that have to

be worn- in by use. All I really wanted to do was to grapple with my reactions to David's death; to think about and discuss the horrendous loss I had sustained; to get into the research for this book in order to understand what was happening to me

Perhaps it does require practice to adjust to new experiences and this will be painful at any time, but the further from David's death I got the easier it became. Whether this occurred because of prior practice or simply because the initial impact of widowhood was receding needs to be researched. But current custom still persists to encourage bereaved people to get on with life as quickly as possible, contrary to medical evidence.

The issue is important because how we deal with the first months of widowhood probably affects the chances for success or failure in the long run.

Coping with the trauma of change

To learn to cope with the increasing impactfulness of modern life it might prove helpful to bring together people who are about to pass through similar life transitions at the same time as, for example, people about to lose a spouse, gain a child, get divorced, move or retire etc. They could be strengthened by others, with whom they can come to share even briefly, some sense of identity. They could see their problems more objectively, trade useful information and insights and suggest future alternatives for one another. They may also form the nucleus for an initial support group after the event occurs which, already having some shared history, may be more effective than such a group starting from scratch. A more successful approach to the formation of widow-to-widow groups may be to initiate their formation where possible *prior* to the onset of widowhood and for seasoned widows to prepare women who know they will soon be widowed prior to the event. I would have had a far easier transition into widowhood had I been counselled to expect and how to handle the panic and paralysing fear that I experienced immediately after David died, rather than the grief I had expected, but which only struck later. I might also have avoided the Takasubo heart attack that I succumbed to several months later had I been counselled that this could happen as a result of profound grief and taken proactive measures to prevent it happening.

Widowhood is becoming an almost universal experience for married women, as the numbers who outlive their husbands continue to increase. 'Old' widows as counsellors for 'new' ones will provide the best support and much needed role models. They should be carefully selected in accordance with their own success in having negotiated the transition to widowhood, general intelligence and social communicative skills. This would also help those doing the counselling by providing a role for widows.

But for lay counselling for widows by widows to succeed, they must first overcome their present reluctance to come to widow groups because of lowered self-esteem, or to become involved in 'widow-work' for fear of making a career of their widowhood. But attempting to deal with challenges of widowhood, instead of denying them, is not a morbid pre-occupation for widows. On the contrary, the very act of thinking objectively about something places us at one remove from it. This applies as much to the helper as to the person being helped. This is a technique of Eastern mysticism which aims at dissociating oneself from one's own suffering. At any rate, as many widows report that the memory of a lost spouse never really leaves one, the successful negotiation of widowhood is not achieved by obliterating the past, but by living the present. By interacting with one another, widows are not prolonging their adjustment to widowhood but attempting to deal with the problems of widowhood precisely so that they can overcome them and stop being obsessed by them. And this could only happen if widows learn to face their widowhood unreservedly until they no longer see themselves and each other as outcasts of society.

Gradualising transitions

Among strategies being suggested to ease the detrimental impact of excessive change is the possibility of 'gradualising' transitions, e.g., retirement should be preceded by a gradually increasing semi-retirement instead of an abrupt all-or-nothing change, like trial marriage before marriage which is already so widely practiced today. Similarly slow induction into the army for new recruits; semi-separation before amicable divorce,

Likewise widows could be gradually transitioned into the living of widowhood. To an extent, this is the aim of many rituals surrounding death - the shorter or longer periods of mourning prescribed by various religions and tribal customs. In Western societies, ritual mourning usually lasts at most up to a month. But adaptation to widowhood can take several years, with two years being the most commonly agreed period. And the fact that widowhood is now so common does not make it any easier to cope with. The successful transition into widowhood requires personal and patient assistance. With modern lifestyles making this support harder and harder to obtain from family and friends, widow-to-widow groups should initiate programs to match suitable 'older' widows with new ones for one-on-one prolonged support.

Social systems for reducing the abruptness of the transition to widowhood should also be devised. Widows could be gradually inducted into independence in slow stepwise increments - in banking, in socialising, in travelling, in being a single guest, in being a single host? Would gradual adaptation to living alone eliminate or reduce the crushing loneliness experienced by widows, many if not most of whom have never before lived alone? Does one need to <u>learn</u> how to live alone rather than being tossed into the deep and left to sink or swim? Would living with relatives, children, friends or in specially devised widows' hostels for the first year, with gradually increasing intervals alone in the widow's own home, allow time to learn how to live on one's own successfully? Some people adapt so successfully to living alone that they would not want to live any other way. But some are devastated by the experience. With the numbers of single households in the post-industrial world increasing rapidly (half the urban population in some cities now lives alone!), this topic should be subjected to intensive investigation. In the meantime, widows who have made this transition successfully should be co-opted to assist in the induction of others.

Increasing pace of change of widowhood

Just as the pace of change in all aspects of life, including lifestyles themselves, is increasing, so too is that of widowhood. Widowhood is not a constant unchanging phenomenon and the rate at which this experience too is changing is increasing in response to other changes in society which affect it.

One of the consequences of the accelerating rate of technological innovation of modern times is the veritable explosion of expanding opportunities for people in all walks of life. The major constraint on most people to taking advantage of these new opportunities is responsibility to others - to a job on which one's livelihood depends or that of one's family, to the care of young children, or aging parents, or an ailing husband.

Widows are probably the freest sector of society. Although the majority of widows view widowhood as a devastating disaster, most still manage to find one redeeming feature in their new situation - independence. Most rate their new-found freedom from responsibility to anyone but themselves as a plus for widowhood.

And after several years many state that they would find it hard to give this up.

The increasing number of lifestyle changes experienced in the modern world and the increasingly transient nature of successive lifestyles are in themselves enlarging the opportunities to widows to find new roles and new social networks and new patterns of living. Today it is possible to become part of a team to work for a year in a disadvantaged country with practically no costs for travel and support; and then to join a university community, live on campus and study practically anything that one wishes for minimal fees. And for no fees at all, one can join local libraries, the University of the Third Age, nature preservation societies. One can choose from an overwhelming array of special tours from retracing the routes of early explorers to studying butterflies in sub-tropical climates. The opportunities open to people today who have the freedom to partake of them, could make kings and queens of former ages envious. But to take advantage of these new opportunities, widows themselves must become aware and responsive to them. 'To stay with it', widows must learn that it is no longer appropriate to use the past as a means of understanding the present. Widowhood in the 21st century his opportunities not even dreamed of in ages past.

But there is also the downside to modern widowhood. Widows will become increasingly more isolated as the average number of children per family continues to fall, because widows in future will have fewer siblings, fewer cousins, fewer children and fewer grandchildren. Also the increasing mobility and transience of relationships will force widows to rely less on their children or neighbours for human intimacy and friendship.

These new 21st century challenges could be countered by developing a network of adopted family members - god-sisters and god-brothers in addition to godchildren. One of the moral obligations of godparents is to become adoptive parents in the event of their godchildren becoming orphaned. In the future, godchildren may well reverse this role to support godparents who have no children of their own and god-sisters and brothers could mutually support each other in widowhood.

The increasing mobility and transience of relationships will force widows to rely less on their children or neighbours for human intimacy and friendship. As serial marriages and serial job changes become more and more common with extending life expectancies, the involvement of widows with children and grandchildren will diminish.

But as accelerating changes in lifestyles affect the whole community, widows in the future will benefit from the continuously increasing opportunities to seek out new experiences and form new relationships with other people who, like themselves, are in transition between old and new lifestyles. *The modern widow needs to be aware that 'pro-active' thinking is as much a buzzword for her today as any other sector of society.*

CHAPTER 5

World without men

There is osteological evidence that pre-historic men lived twenty percent longer than women (Morris, 1997). Although this difference gradually narrowed, life expectancy for men was always greater than for women. Only since the beginning of the twentieth century has this situation reversed and by the close of the twentieth century, life expectancy for women was higher than for men in practically every country in the world. Furthermore, the more technologically advanced the country, the longer women are outliving men. This reversal in life expectancy between men and women has affected widowhood profoundly.

Two major factors normally determine the proportion of women who are widowed in any given society. The first is the difference in the ages to which men and women live (i.e. the difference in life expectancies between the sexes) and the other is the difference in age at which men and women marry, or remarry after divorce or widowhood.

Apart from these two factors, abnormal conditions, such as those arising in pioneering societies or in times of war, or epidemics or famine' can also influence the proportion of women who will be widowed at one time.

Duration of widowhood

There is good evidence that women live five years longer than men due solely to their genetic advantage (Morris, 1997). Comparing samples of nuns and priests, who live similar lives with respect to stress, diet, healthcare etc. it was found that, on average, nuns live five years longer than priests (Morris, 1997). In developing countries, women presently live about four years longer than men. In industrialised societies women currently live six years longer. And in some of the most advanced post-industrial countries, the difference has now reached eight years. This appears to indicate that in developing societies environmental factors reduce women's genetic advantage (currently from five years to four) while in technologically more advanced countries environmental factors are increasing it.

Tables 6, 7 & 8 (see appendix) list three groups of countries, viz., those with life expectancies under sixty years, those with life expectancies of between 60 and 70 years and those with life expectancies over 70 years.

It is immediately evident that the three tables divide, as expected, into underdeveloped, developing and developed (first world) countries. And there is a direct correlation between increasing years of life expectancy and the number of years that women outlive men. *The longer people live; the longer women outlive men.*

In 103 out of the 109 countries listed, life expectancy for men is less than for woman. This is due to the fact that practically every advance in medical science has favoured women more than men.

The fact that the difference in female and male life expectancy also increases with increasing life expectancies, is particularly significant in the present context. If this trend continues, the longer human beings live, the greater the excess of widows will become and the greater the proportion of married women who will be widowed and the longer widowhood with endure.

Those most directly affected by this imbalance are the older people of the population. In Australia (2016 Census), there were 105 females to every 100 males in the total population, but in the population aged 65 and over, there were 379 women to every 100 men. And in the widowed population aged 65 and over, there were 430 widows to every 100 widowers.

In the past the death of a spouse was more or less evenly experienced by men and women. Men died more than women from genetic weakness and from misadventure but this was offset by female deaths in childbirth and weakening due to extended cycles of pregnancies and breast-feeding and by the widespread practice of female infanticide.

Furthermore, as life expectancies for both sexes did not extend beyond what we today call middle-age, the duration of widowhood for both men and women was not extensive, because neither men nor women normally outlived their spouses for long, seldom for more than a few years. Nevertheless, there was usually a surplus of widows in most societies, even when men lived longer than women, because remarriage was encouraged for widowers but discouraged for widows.

There were also periods in history when the excess of widows over widowers was grossly magnified; for example, after big battles when large numbers of young men were killed, or during times of plague or other dangers when women and children were evacuated from urban areas. Conversely, in pioneering eras in newly settled lands such as America in the sixteenth and seventeenth centuries and Australia in the eighteenth century, there were areas where women were in such short supply that no woman would have long remained widowed, unless by choice.

Today it is improving medical knowledge that is steadily increasing the difference in life expectancy between men and women (more than a century after deaths due to childbirth was eliminated as a significant factor in women's life expectancy).

No-one knows why women continue to benefit more from medical advances, although there is much current speculation and research into the subject. It was once thought that men die younger than women because men worked and worried more as providers and protectors. But the entry of women into the workforce has not thus far altered their mortality rates as expected. Whether in paid jobs or not, women still survive better than men at all ages (American Bureau of the Census).

Difference in age between men and women at marriage

Traditionally, women have sought marriage partners who will protect and provide for them especially through the reproductive years of childbearing. This has conditioned them to be attracted to men who are stronger, taller and *older* than themselves. Conversely, men have usually been attracted to women who would appear to need their protection and are therefore, smaller, weaker and *younger* than themselves. And, moreover, as a survival mechanism for the human species , the early marriage of women is highly desirable, while the early marriage of males will make no difference. The reason for this is because males remain fertile almost to the end of their lives, while women cease to be able to reproduce at menopause.

These two considerations explain why, in most societies, at most times, men have married women younger than themselves. Over the past half-century, the average difference in age at first marriage between men and women the USA and Australia narrowed from two and a half to two years (Australian Bureau of Statistics [ABS] Marriages and Divorces, 1996). However, with the unprecedented rise in divorce rates since the middle of the last century, the average difference in age at marriage can now be expected to grow as older widowers and divorced men increasingly find new partners amongst younger generations of divorcees and never married single women.

The highest rates of divorce occur between men and women aged 35-45 years. Divorced men in this age bracket are now able to find new partners or wives in their twenties, usually unencumbered with children from a previous marriage This is happening because of the increasing numbers of young men who are choosing not to marry at all , leaving a surplus of young women without potential partners in their own generation. A major reason many young men are choosing not to marry at all today is because, in this transitional era from industrialised to post-industrialised artificial intelligence-based economies, they fear that that they will not be able to provide for a family. Additionally, as in all societies where females are in excess, they can get all the sex they want outside of marriage. Because of this scarcity of young men available for young women to marry, middle aged divorced men are able to re-marry women much younger than themselves, leaving their middle aged divorced wives, usually with dependent children, with little chance to remarry men of their own generation. Many of these middle-aged divorcees will settle for men usually widowers, much older than themselves.

The net result is a further increase in the average difference in age at marriage between men and women. This in turn will eventually cause further increases in both the numbers of widows and the duration of widowhood.

In an article in Time Magazine (Oct. 1997) entitled 'Mom's Way and My Way', Margaret Carlson, an American journalist said, '[In the 1950's] our dads may have tuned out in their La-Z-Boy recliners, but fewer of them dumped a first family for second wives and second lives'. One reason that fewer of them dumped their first families was undoubtedly that divorce was much rarer and young men were not daunted by rising unemployment rates to remain single and so there were far fewer younger divorcees available to partner. Another was that they did not, on the whole, have as long to get around to it, as life expectancy was a lot shorter.

The older man with a much younger wife has always been accepted by society. It was inevitable in the past, because since the beginning of civilization women commonly died in childbirth. If the second wife also died in childbirth, the third one would be yet further removed in age from her husband. Society has thus been conditioned to accept the old man with a young wife and conversely, to reject the old woman with a young husband (to wit, the media's preoccupation with the unusual phenomenon of Prime Minister Macron of France and his visibly older wife).

However, the practice of older men swapping first wives for second ones of their daughters' generation must now be quite common if those in the public eye are any indication. To list but a few - Dr Spock 80, new wife 40; Nelson Mandela 80, new wife 52; Rupert Murdoch 68, new wife 32; Woody Allen 62, new wife 27; Larry King 63, new wife 37.

There are today in Western countries four times as many widows as widowers and 25% more divorced women as divorced men. Because of the scarcity of male partners for this excess of widows and divorced women, both the proportion of old men who marry young women and the age differences between them can be expected to keep on increasing. Nor is it likely in future, as it was in the past, to be predominantly widowers who are remarrying women decades younger than themselves. If divorce rates continue to climb, it is likely also to be older married men who may tempted to dump old wives for younger available divorced women and progressively younger available widows (as the age gap between men and women at marriage keeps increasing), thus increasing divorce rates still further. This self-perpetuating cycle is in no small measure contributing to the widowhood explosion in first world countries today.

Widowhood in the 21st century

The two distinguishing demographic characteristics of Western populations in the 21st. Century are that they are **ageing** and they are becoming more and more **female** (ABS 2016). Both affect widowhood more acutely than any other phase of the human life cycle.

Today, 16 percent of the population in the Western world is aged over 60. Present projections predict that by 2031, this proportion will rise to 28% There were more men than women in America and Australia until the second half of the twentieth century. The ratio of men to women then reversed and has been decreasing steadily ever since. But even when there were more men than women in these countries, there were always more widows than widowers (see Table 2, Appendix). At the beginning of the twentieth century, widows already outnumbered widowers by almost two to one. By the close of the century, this ratio had increased to almost five to one.

Sex Ratios

In societies where men significantly outnumber women, women can expect to marry well. Being the commodity in short supply, women are sought after, if not fought over, as marriage partners and, therefore, are able to achieve upward economic and social mobility via marriage. Women in such societies do not, usually, pursue other goals in preference to marriage; nor do they actively agitate for personal or political rights. Furthermore, in the past, men, the traditional controllers of social mores, tended to encourage high sexual morality in an effort to keep their wives, in scarce supply, to themselves.

By contrast, societies in which **women are in excess**, such as in all the advanced countries of the Western world today, exhibit trends that are in most respects opposite to these. Upward economic mobility for women through marriage is seldom possible. In fact, the reverse is more likely to occur in which many women, in competition for too few men, have to marry men with less education and earning capacity than themselves.

Women in oversupply tend to feel powerless and devalued and may compensate for these feelings by gaining independence in the workforce and with careers and by agitating for personal and political equality. The Women's Liberation Movement gained its greatest momentum in the mid-1960s and 1970s with the dramatic increase in the excess of available women due to the arrival of baby boomer females at marriageable age (seeking husbands from the smaller cohort of older men which preceded them)

Sociologists have identified two different sources of power governing the relationship between men and women in societies in which there is significant imbalance in the sex ratio. The first is due to *political and economic* domination of one sex over the other. The second is the power due to *scarcity in numbers,* i.e., the power held by the sex in short supply over the other. The former has been named *structural_power* and the latter, *dyadic power* (Grosshand 1992). In the past, structural power was always been held by men in Western society irrespective of which sex was in over or under supply.

Today, the distribution of structural and dyadic power between the sexes has entered a new configuration. Women are now approaching equality in structural power with men for the first time in history. Thus, we now have a situation in which *women and men hold equal structural power but men hold dyadic power*.

This has never happened before and nowhere is this innovation more pronounced than amongst the widowed population. As a class, older widows hold considerable assets today as they usually inherit their husbands' estates in their entireties, but in no other sector of the population is the ratio of men to women lower than that of widowers to widows (currently one widower to every five widows).

How this new socio-demographic pattern is affecting the relationships between the sexes of the widowed population has yet to be investigated. What kind of sexual mores is this society evolving? Do widowers engage in multiple relationships or adulterous ones after they remarry, as is known to occur more frequently in other low sex ratio populations? Are serial partnerships common? Do the women who marry widowers demand and get fidelity from them, controlling their husbands' potential licentiousness with their structural power of wealth or youthfulness (as the wealthier and the more youthful widows and divorcees are those most likely to get new partners)? Or are the remarried widows or divorcees so afraid of losing their husbands or partners that they will share them rather than lose out altogether? In other words, what is the balance of power between these two extremes of dyadic male power and structural female power? Are there in fact any clear cut rules of behaviour or is there rather a prevailing chaos of sexual mores in this new population, with some women holding sufficient structural power to enforce fidelity on their partners in this overly competitive market (perhaps only the very wealthy, the very famous or the very youthful succeed)? Do men married to less wealthy or older widows demand and take more freedom than their partners would want? And are there women in this situation willing to accept polygamous arrangements and others who would rather throw in the towel altogether?

Sex Ratio and Widowhood

The value of commodities in an open market is determined primarily by two factors: the need for that commodity and its availability. A survivor once told me that a loaf of bread during World War II could buy a block of apartments. I have met a widow, reported in the annual list of wealthiest people in Australia to be worth $400,000,000, who explained to me her recent marriage to a 67-year-old widower in the following terms: 'He's kind and considerate and I think he really cares for me. I don't like the packaging but at least he's pleasant and cheerful - and everyone needs to be No. 1 to someone.'

This widow, apart from her enormous wealth, was an attractive and charismatic woman. Her newly acquired husband was a rather dull, rotund gentleman two years her junior and of moderate means. If a woman with her qualifications for marriage is willing to settle for a man whose appearance she disliked simply because 'he's pleasant and cheerful and everyone needs to be No. 1 to someone', then one may reasonably conclude that the serious marriage market for older widows has reached the point of total collapse.

With the growing excess of available women over the last thirty years, boosted now by the arrival of the Baby Boomers at the widowhood years, a new industry has evolved in the quest for male partners; marriage brokers, newspaper-advertising, traditional religious match-makers and, now, the internet are all doing booming business. One has only to compare the 'women seeking men' columns with the 'men seeking women' columns in any newspaper today to see the effect of gender imbalance today. Men invite women decades younger than themselves to reply., while women invite men decades older than themselves to reply.

Older men today have a degree of dyadic power seldom experienced before. They have the opportunity for upward economic mobility and the companionship of women who are more intelligent, more educated, healthier and younger (often by as much as half their own age) than themselves. For the 20% of men who survive their wives, widowerhood in the modern era has become a bonanza.

Baby boomer widows

The baby-boom generation is the excessively large generation born after World War II to compensate for the low birth rates during the war. This generation has carried with it and will continue to do so till the end of its existence, the most significant demographic implications for our society.

The gender imbalance which has so affected widowhood since middle of the 20th century can be expected to greatly intensify with the baby-boom generation now entering the widowhood years. As at every stage of life, from babyhood to widowhood the baby-boom generation has caused a wave. Consequently, as this generation is now entering old age the Western world is experiencing an Age Wave, which is in fact essentially a Widow Wave.

The current arrival of the baby boomers to the widowhood years, added to the two primary factors (modern medicine and difference in age between men and women at marriage) responsible for the increasing proportion of widows and duration of the widowhood is now heralding a widowhood explosion.

CHAPTER 6

Where Have All the Widows Gone

Marginalisation

Among the many new discoveries and surprises of widowhood are the numbers of widows that one suddenly becomes aware of. It is not in the least extraordinary that widows are so numerous , given the demographics of our day. That it comes as a surprise to newly widowed women is the result of society's marginalisation of widows.

'I am just amazed at how many women I meet now who are widows' is an oft repeated discovery amongst new widows. From a seven- year study of 600 widows carried out at the University of California it was concluded that there is a general lack of knowledge about widows 'because in our culture people fear death' (Lieberman, 1996).

Since time immemorial, mankind has feared death and 'striven to wish or magic it away, to play it down, to euphemise it, to try to conceal it from themselves' (Johnson, 1996). The marginalisation of widows is in part this attempt to conceal death from ourselves.

It should be noted that the word 'viduus', the Latin root of the word widow also means apart, set aside, in addition to its alternative meaning of empty.

Throughout history, many societies have striven to deny death by euphemising it with the terminology of life rather than death. Thus, we speak of the 'departed' and of 'passing away'. The word cemetery comes from the Greek meaning a 'sleeping place' and in Hebrew, a cemetery is called a 'house of life'!. These expressions are thousands of years old.

However, the form and intensity of the fear of death has not remained constant. In Victorian times, instead of being tabooed, 'death was magnified, talked about minutely, examined and almost relished' (Johnson, 1996).

But in the post-modern world, death has become the most avoided subject of all, replacing sex as the tabooed topic and the four-letter obscenity as the taboo word of our times.

Little wonder, therefore, that the subject of widowhood is so widely denied today and that widows are so effectively marginalised.

Gail Sheehy in two of the most popular books on the human life cycle, Passages (1976) and New Passages (1995), identifies the modern phases of the life cycle as adolescence (13-20), marriage and family building (20-55), middle age (60-75), golden years (70-85), but she hardly mentions widowhood, a phase which a vast number of women alive today will experience for a period of twenty years and more. We are left with the impression that marriages and coupledom just linger on through middle age and the golden years, blissfully ignoring the fact that over half the women in Sheehy's middle-age and golden years will be widows.

Gail Sheehy (New Passages. 1995) poses a set of rhetorical questions to illustrate the changes challenging our modern society

Do you know how to be 30 and still living with Mom?

Do you know how to be 40 and single and still fulfilled?

Do you know how to be a forced retiree at 50?

Do you know how to be a cancer survivor

Do you know how to be a man today?

BUT NOT - *Do you know how to be to be a widow for 20 years or more?*

And when, in passing, she does refer to widowhood it is as a disease which she classifies, along with cancer and Alzheimer's, as afflictions of old age!!

In a book devoted to the problems of the aging woman (The Change, 1991), Germaine Greer, a guru of the Women's Liberation Movement, makes no more than passing reference to the subject of widowhood in only 10 of its 440 pages. It is hard to imagine how she managed to avoid the subject so successfully in chapters dealing with 'Grief, Sex and The Single Crone', 'The Aged Wife' and 'The Old Witch'. It is as if she is refusing to sympathise with those who brought the burden of widowhood on themselves by succumbing to marriage in the first place. Perhaps, if only unconsciously, she sees widowhood as a punishment for marriage, as others once viewed AIDS as a punishment for homosexuality.

Greer outlines the enormous breadth of current academic publications on women's issues citing more than thirty topics, but nothing on the widowhood of the 10% of all women over the age of fifty who are widows. Her inventory includes: old feminists, new feminists, radical feminists, cultural feminists, gender feminists, feminist critics, feminist collectives, Jewish feminists, lesbian feminists, disabled feminists, feminist nuns, feminist sex workers, feminist sociologists, feminist philosophers, feminist geographers, feminist psychologists. *But no feminist widows! Widowhood, for the Women's Movement, is simply not a feminist issue.*

In Marilyn French's **The War Against Women** (1992), the widow word is absent altogether. When Eva Cox's new book, **Leading Women: Tactics for Making a_Difference**, was published in Australia in 1996, reviewer Wendy McCarthy lauded it on ABC radio as 'at last a package for all of us' - all, that is, except those of us who happen to be widowed. *Widowhood, it would appear, is not a popular topic with the innovative women of our aging society.*

Nor, unbelievably, is it a concern of politicians, with an electorate of almost 10% of all females eligible to vote being widowed! At the conference on the Human Rights of Women held in Melbourne, Australia, on May 21, 1999, there was not a single reference to widowhood. Yet in over 20 years of research about widowhood. I have met precious few widows who have not encountered social discrimination against them

In the media, widowhood is as conspicuous by its absence as in the political and literary arenas. In a recent series entitled 'The Melbourne Woman and the Future' covering an entire page of Melbourne's then leading daily newspaper, **The Age**, for five consecutive days (Feb 10 to Feb 14 1997), not one mention of widowhood was made: singles, marriage, motherhood, employment, aging, sex, fidelity, de facto relationships, feminism and more; everything you could ever want to know about the Melbourne woman and her future except widowhood, when most of Melbourne's women still marry and most of them will one day be widows in that future!

Similarly, in '**Life Matters**' on Australian National radio (October 8, 1997), in a program entitled **Marriage,** the compere, Geraldine Doogue, commented that, 'With today's high rate of divorce (approximately 40%), it is a very brave thing to marry'.

Why then, should a rate of widowhood of 80% not also merit a mention as a hazard of modern marriage?

According *to* **The Jerusalem Post Magazine** review, **Voices,** a new play presented at the 1999 monodrama festival in Israel, dealt with experiences that women have to cope with in a male dominated world, from childhood and everything in between to old age and death. But as usual, no mention of widowhood. In the subconscious minds of both the playwright and the reviewer, most married women must die with their husbands still alive.

In bookstores in London, New York, Washington, San Francisco, Los Angeles, Sydney and Melbourne, I have searched for books dealing with widowhood. Everywhere I have found many popular books about grief and bereavement, but of widowhood, practically nothing.

In one public library, in response to my request for books on widowhood, the librarian on duty produced a single book entitled Transitions: 'The Major Upheavals Most Women Must Face'by Linda P. Viney (1980). Apologising profusely, he said he hoped I would find this single offering helpful. When I pointed out to him, after a short perusal of the book, that although it dealt with finding a life partner, becoming a mother, the empty nest syndrome, illness and death, there was not a single reference in the whole book to widowhood, he embarked upon an exhaustive search for anything about widowhood in the whole library. He came up empty-handed. 'I can't believe it', he said. 'You know, my mother is a widow and she says she's been ostracised and forgotten by society. I'm beginning to think she may be right. I never thought too much about it before'.

When the first branch of Borders, the huge American bookstore, opened in Melbourne in 1998, I made a beeline for the gleaming new emporium, expecting to be able to get a world-wide, up-to-date search of all Borders stores for books on widowhood.

'Good heavens, I can't believe this', came the response from the person behind the information counter. 'What?', I asked. 'There's nothing here!'

One of the major obstacles I have encountered in attempting to deal with the social problem of widowhood is the dismissal by most people, other than widows, of its existence. When members of a victimised group try to express themselves, society often rejects or trivialises their point of view and experiences. Drawing a parallel between an unrecognised victimised group and a well-recognised one can help to break through this barrier of disbelief. Letty Cottin Pogrebin, an expert in non-sexist education, used this kind of parallel therapy by comparing anti-Semitism and woman-hatred (Steinem, 1992). The main characteristics which set widows at odds with society are their association with death and their anomalous sexual situation. Drawing parallels on these two dimensions between widows and Jews may, by comparison, demonstrate how widows too have been discriminated against.

Jews have been associated with death, both as perpetrators and as victims.

As perpetrators they have been branded as killers of Christ, poisoners of drinking wells, disseminators of the Black Plague, ritual murderers of Christian children and more. As victims they are seen, somewhat more realistically, as a persecuted people murdered across the centuries in innumerable pogroms culminating in the Holocaust in the 20th century.

Widows have similarly been perceived as both perpetrators and victims. By the defining event of their identity, the demise of their husbands, widows are closely associated with death. Because of this, in many primitive cultures, they have been and still are, physically distanced from the community to avoid spiritual and physical contagion. They have been seen at various times as responsible for the deaths of their husbands, either actively by murdering them

or passively by neglecting them, or simply by association, as bear-
ers of ill-fortune. As victims they have been burnt in the funeral
pyres of their husbands in retribution for their sins in a former incarnation or as witches for their perpetration of evil in this life.

Sexually, Jews and widows have both been stereotyped as voluptuous predators, the Jew raping pure Christian maidens in the
Middle Ages, contaminating Aryan genes in Hitler's Germany, or
spreading AIDS in Thailand when the economy crashed in 1997.
Widows have been seen as sexually explosive due to deprivation,
waiting to devour any available male or unsuspecting wife's husband. As victims, again more realistically, Jewish women have
been raped across the centuries, resulting in many a fair skinned,
green-eyed or red-haired Jewish descendant; widows were so
commonly raped in ancient times that special laws were enacted
to defend them against this abuse and, today, the abuse of widows
by unscrupulous men who take advantage of their sexual vulnerability is a common focus of rap sessions in widow-to-widow
groups.

Widows, like Jews, are also depicted as either too strong or too
weak or too rich or too poor. Jews are at times believed to control
the banks, the media and even governments via the secret activities
of the Elders of Zion. But they are also seen as impoverished ref-
ugees threatening the countries they infiltrate no matter how many
arrive with skills and wealth; they were at times differentially
taxed and unfairly excluded from higher centres of learning, promotion in legal, political and military careers and social clubs.
Widows have similarly been viewed as both wealthy and powerful
or impoverished and helpless. 'Widows are all rich,' says the Oxford Dictionary of Proverbs. 'Worldwide, widows are poor', says
Sally Cline (Lifting the Taboo, 1995). The truth is that neither Judaism nor widowhood is confined to any socio-economic class. It
is apparent from these comparisons with the prejudices against

Jews, an indisputably victimised group in the past, that *society does indeed victimise widows today*.

Because both Jews and widows are discriminated groups, the lessons I learnt on becoming a widow mirrored those I had been taught as the child of Jewish immigrants to Australia in the 1930s: that the world is divided into us and them; to survive, we must put a protective ring of secrecy around ourselves; never to reveal our inner secrets; to keep a low profile so that maybe 'they' will forget that we exist. In closed widow groups and now also on the Widownet website, widows speak only to one another of these matters in their struggle to come to grips with their rejection by society.

'No-one wants to hear about grief for long. No one really even wants to see you because you remind them of what will one day happen to them' is a commonly heard complaint from new widows.

So widows soon learn to hide their widowhood and speak only to one another of their new bewildering experiences.

Minority groups that are discriminated against often band together and sublimate the discrimination against them, convincing themselves that they are better than everyone else. But widows usually become widowed suddenly and quite late in life. They don't have the resources to counter bigotry as do people who have been discriminated against since birth. So they often take the alternative route of trying to escape by disassociating themselves from the group. They go into hiding, thus aiding and abetting society's denial of them.

'I hate being seen with hordes of other women in public, because people know that you are widows' one widow said in a group session and she was one of the minority that even get as far as attending a support group. Many widows will not attend widow support groups because they don't like to be identified as widows. There is little comfort for them in the company of other widows if they have assimilated society's denigration of them. Associating with other widows is seen as forced upon them for lack of other better company, rather than by choice and so leads to further lowering of self-esteem.

To overcome their relegation to the fringes of society, widows will first have to overcome their own loss of self-esteem in order to 'come out' and claim a place in society, as so many other hitherto denied groups have done in the last few decades.

As a first step, joining a widow's group should be turned into a privilege---a closed society with rewards for membership. Today, people celebrate turning 65 in our society because this entitles them to a senior citizen card which carries privileges with it. Widowed people form a large enough sector of society to create advantages for themselves. Other smaller sectors of the population have clubs which one is privileged to join - nature-lovers, telecommunication workers, owners of antique cars, hoteliers, students, seniors, etc. Many achieve even greater rewards by organising internationally so that their privileges extend worldwide and escalate in magnitude as their numbers multiply. A widows' movement with a membership of millions could open up opportunities for employment, housing, travel, cheaper living, visibility in advertising and marketing, widows' legal services and banking services, etc.

At present, there is a slow awakening to the financial implications of this growing market. Prue Goward, the chief women's adviser to the Australian government in 1995 drew attention to the fact that on average, women of retirement age have less than half as much invested in superannuation assets as men. Overall, men hold 2.7 times the super assets of women. Super fund companies should be targeting women to counter this lingering anomaly. Both life insurance and superannuation were, in the past, regarded as buffers against the inability of men to provide for their families. As women are now outliving men by an average of six to eight years in those countries that have superannuation funds, it has become more and more anomalous that women should continue to be less involved in super funding than men. As women become progressively more likely to be the final supporters of families and themselves, life insurance companies such as the Life and Health Insurance Foundation, are beginning to target wives rather than their husbands. Similarly, with health insurance, many jobs today provide health insurance cover for the dependents of men who then lose this coverage if the husband dies. With current mortality statistics, it would make more sense to cover the families of wives who work and better for women to claim head-of-family status in policies of all kinds which also extend benefits to their families.

This tentative beginning could be expected to burst into an active competitive market once the blackout on widowhood is lifted. I visualise services to fill the myriad needs of widows, especially new widows once they have emerged from the initial years of mourning. I envisage advertisements in women's magazines such as:

Widowed? We can offer you a comprehensive group of services to help you through this difficult period.

Widowed? You need a new image, why not start with a makeover. We can help you to the new life you now need to find.

Widowed? You may need to relocate, downsize your car, rethink your investments. We have a team of experts who have specialised in the problems that widowhood brings. Let us help you.

Widowed and wanting a break? We have specialised in putting together widow packages which will be socially and economically advantageous to widowed people.

Widows could themselves staff housing projects, travel agencies for widowed people and organisations for widowed volunteers, etc. They could achieve class representation in the fight to eliminate financial discrimination against singles. They could campaign for financial advantages in group participation, e.g., in travel, in insurance, in supermarkets. They could have a voice in the planning of new housing projects which are currently governed mainly by the profit motive, resulting in housing units which are too small for comfort and too expensive for most to afford.

Widows who controlled their own destinies, who were self-reliant and determined their own visibility would soon no longer be denigrated, marginalised or denied.

CHAPTER 7

Widow-Phobia

". . . be wery careful o' vidders all your life." **Charles Dickens Pickwick Papers.**

Stereotyping of widows

The association of the widow with sex and death, have made her a prime target for stereotyping and tabooing throughout history. Two French idioms strongly reflect this heritage: 'Madame Veuve Lorraine' (literally, the Widow Lorraine) is a colloquial expression meaning the guillotine and 'la veuve poignet' (literally, the widow's wrist) is French slang for male masturbation.

People who are different from the majority are often stereotyped. This enables those who feel threatened by their existence to focus their ill-defined anxiety in order to allay it. Therefore, stereotypes are often ascribed contradictory characteristics so as to encompass all of the members of the population being stereotyped.

Thus, widows are seen as richer and poorer, stronger and weaker, more sexy and less sexy, happier and sadder, more holy and more evil than the rest of society. "Widows are always rich" is the only entry under widowhood in the **Penguin Dictionary of Proverbs (2001)**. "Worldwide, widows are poor" said Sally Cline (1995). The dichotomy of strength and weakness in the widow's image derives from the removal of male guardianship. With the death of her husband, a woman gains freedom and independence.. The empowered female has always been a threat to male-dominated societies. This led to the burning of widows at the stake in the Middle Ages But at the same time, she loses male protection, and so more often, the widow has been seen as weak, ineffective, diminished.

Because they are sexually deprived mature women, widows are depicted as being both oversexed and undersexed. 'He who wooeth a widow must go stiff before' was a popular proverb in Renaissance England. A hundred years later, Charles Dickens wrote 'Take example of your father, my boy and be wery careful of vidders all your life'. But in stark contrast to these depictions of the widow as sexually depraved , the Christian Bible saw the widow as a bride of Christ, in a state of grace, because of her acquired celibacy.

In literature, the widow has been depicted as both joyous, the merry widow blossoming in her new-found freedom and defeated, crushed and pitiful. 'Do like other widows – buy yourself widows weeds and be cheerful' and, 'The comfortable estate of widowhood is the only hope that keeps up a wife's spirits', wrote John Gay in the Beggars Opera at the beginning of the eighteenth century. But the depiction of widowhood portrayed in Homer's **Hector and Andromede**, (quoted on page 23), is one of irredeemable doom.

Widows in the form of old women or grannies have been a common feature of children's fairytales since time immemorial. In these stories, widows have been paradigms of both good and evil, safety and danger. Little Red Riding Hood, Snow White and the Seven Dwarfs, Rapunzel, Sleeping Beauty, Hansel and Gretel, The Wizard of Oz all feature an old, unattached woman. Most old women who are alone are widows and, therefore, old single women are usually perceived as widowed. Lord Desart, in an essay entitled 'Mock Sermon on Old Mother Hubbard' written in the latter years of the nineteenth century, made this assumption clear:

'Mother Hubbard . . . was old [and] there being no mention of others, we may presume she was alone, a friendless old solitary widow. Yet did she despair . . . No! She went to the cupboard'.
(Penguin Dictionary of Quotations (1960)

It is interesting, incidentally, to note the accretion of stereotypes in Lord Desart's own perception of widows. He not only tells us that because Mother Hubbard is old and alone, she is probably a widow, but, without evidence from the story, he also assumes that she is friendless. And he then goes on to pigeon-hole her into yet another stereotyped image; being a widow, we would expect her to despair.

The disease of widowhood

Susan Sontag, in her famous essay on 'Illness as Metaphor', says, 'any important disease whose causality is murky and for which treatment is ineffectual, tends to be awash with significance' (1977). Sontag uses as examples, how tuberculosis in the nineteenth century and cancer in the twentieth century were turned into metaphors. As long as its cause was unknown and treatment ineffectual, tuberculosis was regarded as the manifestation of passion which was frustrated from natural expression by circumstance or the individual's personality. Tuberculosis became the metaphoric equivalent of delicacy, sensitivity, sadness, powerlessness. Cancer has, in the twentieth century, been similarly regarded as a disease of passion, caused by repression rather than frustration. Sontag argues that cancer has become a metaphor for ruthlessness and implacability, for example, 'terrorism is a cancer in modern society 'Thus, in the nineteenth century, disease became a reflection of character under the control of the patient's will and this concept led to the twentieth century notion of the emotional causes of disease.

Historically, many diseases have been metaphorised in their times. In the Middle Ages, the leper was the emblem of corruption and decay. First the disease itself becomes a metaphor. Then the name of the disease is imposed on other things. The disease becomes adjectival---leprous came to mean disgusting or ugly; pestilent, from 'pestilence' which was originally the name for bubonic plague, came to mean injurious to religion, morals or public peace in 1513; pestilential then entered the language as meaning pernicious in 1531; cankerous, which was another word for cancer, came to mean corroding in 1691 and now cancerous means a spreading evil corruption.

'Nothing,' says Sontag, 'is more punitive than to give a disease a figurative meaning, because this soon acquires moralistic responsibility and guilt which is then attached to the sufferer'.

The acquired figurative meaning then spreads from the diseases to the victims of these diseases and, finally, from the victims to those closely associated with them. Of all human associations, that of husband and wife, who in the Judeo-Christian tradition are regarded as 'one flesh', is the closest and fear of the contagion of death from the deceased spouse, has ascribed to widowhood traces of the quality of a disease. Thus, in the Bible, widows were classed with lepers. Three thousand years later, widowhood is still being grouped with Alzheimer's disease and cancer (Sheehy, 1995). In India still today, acne is believed to come from sexual intercourse with a widow (Holt, 1999).

Furthermore, as with classic diseases, widows have also assumed part of the revulsion and guilt associated with death and disease. In many diverse cultures, the wife who outlives her husband is thought to be in some way responsible for his death. In the Judeo-Christian tradition, death, especially premature death, was considered to be a punishment by God and, by association, the widow assumed at least part of the guilt. This is reflected in such phrases in the Bible as: *'the reproach of widowhood' (Isaiah 54:4)*

And the utterances of the widow Ruth . 6h: *'the hand of Yahweh (God) has been raised against me' (Ruth 1:14)*

'Shaddai (God) has marred me bitterly' (Ruth 1:20)

'Yahweh has given witness against me and Shaddai has afflicted me' (Ruth 1:21).

In India, suttee was the result of a religious teaching that the husband's death was the widow's fault because of her sins in a former incarnation.

It is interesting to note that in early Christian times widows were believed to be endowed with supernatural healing powers and given a role in ministering to the sick by the laying on of hands - precisely the opposite of this perception of their complicity in the death of their husbands.

Once the victim is implicated in the cause of his or her illness, the disease can be brought under human control and this is the value of metaphorising illness. For example, in plague-ridden Europe in the late sixteenth and seventeenth centuries, it was widely believed a happy person would not get the plague. In the nineteenth century, the unfrustrated person was thought to be protected from tuberculosis. In the early twentieth century, it was thought that the unrepressed person would not get cancer. So to avoid these dreaded diseases one could at least now try to do something positive, like being happy, unfrustrated or unrepressed.

Widowhood is the ultimately incurable disease and has been metaphorised like any other incurable illness. However the purpose of metaphorising physical diseases like leprosy, bubonic plague, tuberculosis and cancer, to bring these diseases under apparent human control could not apply to the disease of widowhood which is caused by *someone else's* death. Widows are thus burdened with the metaphor but not the benefit. They cannot avoid the disease by doing anything.

Morton Lieberman, a psychiatrist who has worked extensively with widows, has challenged the concept of widowhood as a disease (Lieberman, 1996). He justifiably believes that his colleagues are counterproductive in treating widows with therapy and tranquillisers and judging their success by the time it takes a widow to snap back and act her old self again. Firstly, a new widow cannot ever be her old self again and, secondly, she is not suffering from an illness. She does not need to 'recover' from her affliction to become whole again. She has instead to negotiate the transition to a new phase in life, just as she did in moving from adolescence to adulthood (with all its difficulties) and all the other life transitions she has already negotiated. But whereas all the other transitions for Shakespeare's Seven stages of life have been well researched there has been little, if any, academic research of the transition from married life to widowhood. What is desperately needed is a better understanding of the process of this transition: the initial phases of shock and terror followed by grief ; the eventual slow orientation to the widow's new position in society as a single woman and finally the search for a new productive role in this, the eighth and final stage of life .

Symbolism of widowhood

Widowhood has also been contaminated with the fear of uncontrollable female sexuality. This has made of the widow a powerful symbol of chaos and destruction. She is seen as voluptuous but sexually thwarted, harbouring a mounting frustration which must eventually find an outlet in the destruction of someone else's marriage or destroy her - the blueprint of a vampire! This may be one of the subconscious factors leading to the connection of widows with witches.

Originally, witches were not considered to be evil, but the growing independence of women in the Middle Ages was stopped, first by making witchcraft evil, then, by making most witches female (whereas formerly witches were male or female) and finally burning them at the stake, thus getting rid of the leaders of female insurrections. As these were mainly older women, in the popular imagination witches then became older feeble-minded women who lived alone and inflicted harm (whereas formerly, they had done good, acting as healers and administering herbs and medicines).

Thus widows and witches came to share many characteristics. Firstly, as older women, many witches would in fact have been widows. Widows today, like witches in the past, usually live alone; both have been seen historically first as possessing healing powers and later as capable of inflicting harm, both have been believed to possess supernatural powers and both have at times been burnt at the stake.

It is difficult to prove claims about subconscious phenomena. Often the best one can do is to offer conjectural evidence. Rolf Brenner (1995), in a study of widows in Anglo-Saxon England, cites one story in which a widow 'who has murder on her mind . . . practiced black magic to further her interests as a widow' and another in which a witch and a widow act together as accomplices in an exploit for William the Conqueror. 'Is it surprising to find the two together?' he asks. In conclusion, Brenner points out that 'three out of the only five recorded cases against witches in Anglo-Saxon England were widows.

Germaine Greer also saw the connection between widows and witches. In her book **The Change** (1991), she wrote, 'Though young men and women have (also) been accused of sorcery . . . the archetypal witch is both old and female.

The association of widows with witches spans many cultures. In India, Hindu widows, no longer burned on the funeral pyre since the practice of suttee was outlawed by the British in 1829, are now social outcasts, 'spurned as witches both by their own families and society generally' (Morris, 1997). This is the plight of millions of women since 50% of all women over 50 years of age are widowed in India.

Similarly, in Nigeria women were often accused of witchcraft on the death of their husbands (Hackett, 1985).

As I researched the literature for this book. I came more and more to feel the connection between widows and witches - the unspoken taint of evil, an inescapable whiff of doom. My own experienced evidence of this connection is worth reporting here. The first was an impromptu witch's incantation, performed by my daughter's thirty-five year old close friend who had recently lost her young husband to a heart attack. Suddenly, out of the blue one hot summer's evening she gathered her three children around her and mockingly began performing a witch's jig around an imaginary fire. 'That's me now', she screeched, 'A witch, a witch, I'm a witch. Beware!'

My other bizarre experience of the connection between widows and witches occurred in a Borders bookstore in Washington, USA I had asked the attendant at the inquiry desk to search the computer catalogue for any books containing the word 'widow' in the title. This was my usual practice in bookstores since I began work on this book. Usually, I would get about ten references, eight of which were irrelevant. On this occasion, reams of paper started issuing forth from the printer, unravelling like a snake, on and on, out onto the floor beyond the counter. 'What on earth have you done?', I exclaimed. 'Did you cross-reference 'widow' with another word perhaps?'. 'No ma'am', replied the bewildered youth, 'I just typed in **"witches"** like you said!'

Taboo in widowhood

Because of the deep fear it arouses, widowhood is a tabooed subject in many societies. Sally Cline, in her book on death and dying, writes: 'Choosing to write about death is choosing to be looked on as a freak - a worthy freak, but still a freak. Choosing to talk about writing about death ... is asking to be silenced' (Cline S 1995).

I could write this paragraph substituting the word "widowhood" for "death" as an exact description of my own experience in writing this book.

It became part of my research to broach the subject with as many people as possible and observe their responses. Some would simply make no comment, stare for a split second and change the subject. Some would make some inane, embarrassed remark like 'How nice', 'Oh, really', 'How interesting' and then change the subject. A few expressed distaste: 'How morbid; should you really be prolonging your mourning like this?' 'Aren't you making a profession of widowhood?

Cline continues, 'In the past . (society did not attempt to) exclude or invisibilise (the bereaved) as we do today. We offered a respect for mourners and gave them formal mourning time [but today] grief has a shelf-life and a talk-by date'.

This delegitimisation of public grief has contributed, amongst a host of other factors, to the marginalisation of widows and tabooing of the subject of widowhood.

In some Australian Aboriginal tribes, widows and widowers are physically distanced from the community because their presence is deemed unlucky - either by contagion with death or because the familiar sound of their voices may attract the spirits of their dead spouses to the community. In the past, they were sometimes condemned to silence, often for years. In Nigeria, one of the customs that Church missionaries tried to abolish was that of 'compelling widows to remain in seclusion for several years' after the death of a spouse (Hackett, 1985). Astoundingly, the Hebrew words for widow and widower, 'Almanah' and 'Alman' respectively, come from the word 'Ilem' meaning 'dumb,' although the reason for this connection has been lost in history. The marginalisation of widows is due to a variety of reasons, but one reason is undoubtedly the legacy of these primitive taboos.

In modern Western countries, widows are simply kept out of mainstream society. Lynne Caine (1974) called them 'an underground current . . . swirling beneath the surface of society', Jeanette Kupfermann (1992) called them 'a forgotten regiment of women' and Sally Cline (1995), called them 'a rising population of outcasts'.

Widows are still feared as omens of bad luck and shunned as insalubrious. For example, there is still today an Indian myth that acne in men is caused by sex with widows (or animals) in a previous incarnation. Women twice widowed are still considered risks for a third marriage by many modern Jews (a legacy from the Biblical story of Tamar). 'People treat women differently when they find out that their spouse has died, as if they can see the Grim Reaper peaking over the widow's shoulder' wrote Morton Lieberman (1996). And, above all, widows remain reminders to wives of what probably awaits them. *As harbingers of death, widows have in the past been kept at a distance by physical exclusion, silencing, killing and now by marginalising.*

We have indeed inherited a formidable culture of widow-phobia.

Throughout this book widows have been associated with a dizzying array of negative attributes - chaos and destruction, bad luck, emptiness, feeble-mindedness, nymphomania, asexuality, loss of legitimacy, loss of humanity, unwholesomeness, unnaturalness, transmitters of disease, potential murderesses, harbingers of death and doom. *For widowhood to become a positive experience it will have to first be detoxified of the accretions of centuries of meta-phorization, symbolism and taboo.*

Not surprisingly, widowers have never been vilified because they have never been viewed as threats to the social order. Remarkably, even when women died extensively in childbirth, widowers do not appear to have been held responsible for their wives' deaths even though it might be argued that they were, in fact, involved in these mortalities.

It is remarkable that in the now vast literature on the discrimination against women by society, the glaring discrimination against women evidenced by the differential treatment of widows and widowers has so rarely been questioned.

CHAPTER 8

'No more dinners, only lunches'

This chapter on the etiquette of coupledom has been in and out of this book twice. When I first submitted it to my editor Aviva Layton in Los Angeles, she laughed me out of the room. 'What nonsense', she cried. 'This is the 21st century. Maybe in the 'burbs' of Melbourne people still carry on like that, but not here in LA. I don't know the marital status of someone sitting next to me at a dinner party - and I couldn't care less'.

I argued with her vehemently at first. The fact that widows are not invited to couple activities such as dinner parties is a major issue for widows. In my experience every new widow complains of the hurt and sheer loneliness of suddenly being marginalised from her previous social circle of married friends.

Then my editor changed ground. 'Even if it is true, it will trivialise the book'. My thirty-eight year old daughter Debbie supported her. 'That may be what happens in your generation, but certainly not in mine'.

I finally gave way and removed the essay from the manuscript. Several months later, Debbie told me that she had been invited to a dinner party of older people. 'Mum, it's true - all the widows were bunched up at one end of the table, just as you described. The atmosphere was strained and no-one really enjoyed themselves'. I discussed it with the hostess and she told me that so many of her circle of friends were now widowed that she held a 'mixed' dinner once a month to which she invited both widows and couples.

Some weeks later, Debbie burst into my study waving an article she had extracted from the New York Times entitled 'Get Me Outta Here', written by one Monica Yazigi. The theme was the difficulty New York hosts were experiencing in getting enough men to balance the sexes at their dinner parties. Unbelievably, the author claimed that even gays demanded equal representation of the sexes. '(Dinner) hosts almost invariably say that whether their guests are married or single, gay or straight, dinner parties ought to have equal representation of the sexes'. And this was the Big Apple - not the 'burbs' of Melbourne !

Finally, about a month later I got a call from Aviva in LA. She had been telling a colleague about my book and mentioned the controversy over the 'ridiculous' dinner party article. Her friend, who happened to be a divorcee, reacted by telling her to have me to reinstate the chapter at once!

I myself had been unaware of this particular social discrimination before I myself experienced it , and from the initial reactions of my editor, herself a married woman of my generation and of my daughter, it would appear that this is a little recognised widows' problem, which widows keep to themselves. But their exclusion from social gatherings to which only couples are invited is discussed in most widow-group encounters. This rejection is so obvious and immediate that no widow who once had a social circle of married friends fails to notice it. Understandably, they feel hurt and rejected when they discover, as they inevitably do, that events in homes to which they would formerly have been invited are now happening without them. This is no trivial matter. As formerly married women they had probably socialised mainly with other married couples. Now, when they most need their friends, they are either dropped completely, or at least realigned within the only social network they had.

Widows are witnesses to the future for married couples and so it is less threatening to keep them out of couple society and reassign them to mid-day luncheons, or afternoon cinema showings and morning bridge sessions. Widows can continue to function in mainstream society as long as they are not too clearly defined as widowed. But as soon as the missing half of an erstwhile couple comes into focus – at dinner parties, couple excursions, holidays – the widow is an unwelcome, insidious reminder of what awaits all married couples.

The dinner party is the high altar of the culture of coupledom and is governed by a complex set of rules. Most of us who have lived in that world have acquired them unconsciously in the early years of marriage. With a little experience and by learning from others more advanced along life's path, one soon learnt, for instance, that one can visit the host's toilet, but not open the fridge to see what the next course is; one can criticise a new piece of furniture, but not the cooking. If there are six at a table, the host and hostess sit at either end and the guests either side, either husband and wife side-by-side or swapped, but never two women and two men on the same side. No matter how many couples are invited, this pattern of alternating men and women can be followed. If the total even number present divided by two ends up an odd number, there will always be females either side of the host and males either side of the hostess. But if it ends up an even number (e.g., 8 divided by 2), there will always be one female adjacent to the hostess and one male adjacent to the host. This is totally acceptable. I was never aware of any hostess seeking to avoid it.

But if a widow is invited, one female is going to have to end up next to another female. Whether or not that female is the widow has significance for widows. Placed there, I feel the odd one out, the usurper of the natural order. When I had a husband and for some reason he was not there, it didn't mean a thing to me where I sat. But as a widow, where I am seated has become a sign to me now of my social status and the sensitivity and awareness of the hostess.

If there is more than one widow, the problem becomes grossly compounded. It comes down to three alternatives: allocating the men to the wives and isolating the widows from male company; allocating the husbands to the widows and isolating the wives or mixing the wives and widows in the allocating and isolating process. All three are disastrous to someone. The first will raise obvious resentment, if not trepidation, among the wives; the second highlights the widows as deprived women; the third will necessitate treating the widows unequally, which will involve further discrimination.

I had a particularly vivid experience of this new significance in seating arrangements when a friend who had just been through a gruelling divorce invited a group of people who had each in some way helped her through the protracted proceedings. She had booked a long narrow table for eleven people at a restaurant to celebrate. The group consisted of four married couples, the hostess herself now a single as a divorcee, myself and another widow. The hostess flushed and excited by her victory in court and completely inexperienced in the problems of singles and marrieds at dinner parties rushed to seat her guests without planning. She placed herself at the top of the table and instinctively seated two married couples on either side of her, leaving the two widows to be seated at the end facing each other. She fumbled and blushed, not knowing how to complete the seating. Totally vexed at the sight of the two left over widows, she tried separating them by placing my fellow widow at the end of the long table and inviting me to double up with her at the head of the table. I refused the invitation because of the hurt, it would have caused my fellow widow to be left alone at the opposite end of the table. I was cut to the core by this stupid, irrational predicament. Had David been alive I would have been 'up there' with the other 'heavy weights. As it was, I would now henceforth forever be 'down here' with the other misfits in the celebrations of life.

Amongst older social groups, as the proportion of widows increases, dinner parties begin to divide into nights for marrieds only and mixed parties which means widows are also invited. Widows resent this accommodation almost as much as not being invited at all. They see themselves as second-class women to those who still have husbands and this division of married and mixed socialising only accentuates their loss of status. It soon became obvious to me that there was not much future for widows in couple dinner parties.

It is difficult to understand the dogged adherence to such an outdated convention. 'What is wrong', Monica Yazigi asks, in the **Time Magazine** article, 'with unbalanced tables at this late date in the twentieth century, when almost every other social convention has been undermined?' The answer she finds amongst her New York hosts and hostesses is 'the mild sexual tension that ensues even among happily married couples'.

But I don't agree. I don't think one needs to equalize the gender numbers to elicit mild sexual tension and furthermore I think a good case could be made for widows injecting quite a healthy dose of sexual tension into any dinner party!

The dinner party is often the first unmistakably encountered instance of social exclusion of the widow from couple society. But there are myriads of other activities, often derivatives of this basic one. For example, widows cease to be invited by couples to holiday weekends, or more extended vacations at winter or summer holiday resorts, or trips overseas. These, of course, will all entail repeated dinners together.

However, if the focus of the activity is not primarily social, such as study weekends or trips with an educational theme, party political support activities etc. then the mixing of couples and singles becomes acceptable and eating arrangements present no problem.

Margaret Mead saw the separation of married and single persons as a social problem almost a century ago, long before the acute shortage of men in the extended years of living today. Mead said, 'I think that family living will become increasingly narrow, cramped and frustrating unless married couples open the doors of their homes and bring some singles into their lives'. Interestingly, Mead saw the problem then as one of deprivation for married people, exactly the reverse of how it is seen today. Opening the doors of friendship to the widowed, the divorced and the never-married 'would bring a family relief from [boredom] through the diversity of other views and other interests', she claimed.

Mead did not mention what benefit this breakdown of barriers between single and married people might offer to singles. Nor did she suggest that singles may open their doors to married people. The assumption was and still is, that married couples are the custodians of hospitality, the initiators of social invitations. There is no reason for these assumptions. They are simply the legacy of centuries of custom and convention.

In societies where over 50 per cent of adult people now live alone, it is time these mores changed. It is intolerable that because a woman loses (or divorces) her husband, she should be dropped by her social network. It is cruel and extremely damaging. Social isolation at any time can have very serious repercussions and coming hard on bereavement it is likely to result in clinical depression.

People have a social responsibility to each other in civilised societies and it is hard to imagine a more basic one than that of friends to a bereaved wife. Yet this is the very bond which is so cruelly ruptured in widowhood for totally irrational and outmoded reasons. It is ironic that very often good people who go out of their way to be kind and helpful are, in reality, the source of a great deal of harm and suffering to new widows because they are insensitive to this diabolical ejection of the widow from her former social milieu. *The etiquette of coupledom is in dire need of revision.*

CHAPTER 9

Single again

Celibacy

In the past, widows were generally expected to be celibate after their husbands died and since they were discouraged from remarrying in most cultures, widows usually expected to bury their sex lives along with their husbands.

In Ancient Rome, Ovid called older women who did not behave chastely 'wanton hags' and this was considered the ultimate censure - a slut, trash, trollop. In the Middle Ages, the standard formula in wills leaving a stipend to a wife stated that it should continue only if she remained chaste. In the fourteenth century in England, Chaucer mocked the widow who did not behave chastely. There was even a formal statutory Church document for widows to complete in the presence of the diocese bishop, avowing their faithfulness to their deceased husbands for the rest of their lives. In an account of the life of Elinor de Montford, widow of the Earl of Leicester and her governess, Cecily de Stanford, both women were recorded as having taken vows of chastity to their deceased husbands before the Archbishop of Canterbury whereby 'the two women put on wedding rings to symbolise their marriage to Christ' (Gies & Gies, 1980).

Before the twentieth century, celibacy was considered a virtue and in early Christian times celibates were revered and accorded special privileges; until very recently and even today in many cultures, widows were expected to remain celibate for the rest of their lives, unless they remarried.

'Cross-culturally . . . celibacy [is] intertwined with ideas of widowhood', wrote Sally Cline (1979). To guard their virtue, in many cultures, widows are still expected to withdraw from society. In Japan, to ensure faithfulness to her dead spouse, a widow is forbidden to take any interest in anyone outside her family. The black dress of widows in Mediterranean countries, worn until they die or remarry, sends out the message to stay away - the message that widows are the sexual property of dead husbands. (It is interesting to note that in these same Mediterranean countries if men dress in black at all, it is seldom for any longer than a few days after spousal bereavement.)

In the twentieth century in Western cultures, the ancient reverence for celibates was reversed. Today, adults who are celibate are seen as aberrant and somehow deficient and genital activity is considered normal and necessary for health and happiness. Widows are therefore under social pressure to find a new relationship , not only to avoid singledom, but also for their physical and psychological well-being.

But finding a new sexual partner is not an easy undertaking for women in widowhood. Quite apart from the scarcity of available males, courtship for widows is more complicated than for other women. Today men often expect women to make the first approach if they are interested in a sexual relationship. Because of this, it may even be inferred that if a woman does not take the initiative, she is not interested. But any initiative on the part of a widow, for any reason, is also likely to be seen as an attack and the man approached may feel threatened because of the enormous numerical disparity between older men and women. I myself personally experienced such an embarrassing encounter some years into my widowhood. I was arranging a dinner party for friends that

I had met at a current affairs class run by the University of the Third Age which I had been attending regularly for some years. A few of us had by now become good friends and felt very much at ease with each other and I had decided it was time to arrange a dinner party for my own circle of friends. At the end of a Current Affairs session I approached each of my chosen guests asking if they were free to come to dinner at my place on such and such a date. The response I got from one of the male guests was not "thank you very much. I am free on that date" or "thank you very much, but I am not free on that date". To my horror, he answered "thank you very much, but I *have a partner*". I was mortified and disgusted by the implication of his response. I replied that I was not inviting him into my bedroom but to my dining room. and walked away angry and humiliated.

Widows are, not surprisingly, often perplexed by their disrupted sexual lives. Widowhood forces them to deal with their sexuality anew and widows would do well to seriously consider the issue of their truncated sexual lives rather than rushing headlong into new and often damaging relationships.

Most will have emerged from a sexual relationship which had long ago become routine. Now that this has disappeared the widow needs to reassess her own sexuality. What are her real sexual needs without regard to anyone else's, or the expectations of society? How have the passing years changed her since she last had actively to seek out a sexual partner? How will she deal with the moral issues of lesbianism and adultery which she will probably soon encounter should she decide to search for a new sexual partner in a social environment in which available women grossly outnumber men? Can she successfully adjust to the possibility of never again entering a sexual relationship as will probably be the case for many widows given the harsh demographic realities of our times?

The sexual relationship a widow had with her husband before his death will profoundly affect her sexuality in widowhood. Some widows may be happy to be released from sexual activity sustained mainly to please the husband. Some may have had little or no sexual relations with their husbands for years and will therefore be little affected by widowhood in this matter. And others, who never before had been abstinent long enough to feel it, will find total deprivation frustrating.

How the husband died can also be expected to affect sexuality in widowhood. A widow who has watched her husband slowly transformed physically into another person by the ravages of a terminal disease will be affected very differently by his death, to one whose husband walked out the door one morning, a healthy and sexually active man, never to return from an accident or sudden heart attack.

Little is known of how widows react sexually to widowhood. There are reports of increased libido in women immediately after bereavement (Lieberman, 1996). This may be the response to panic at losing the sexual partner, or some deep Freudian psychological association between sex and death. Dr. David Reuben claims in his best-seller "Any Woman Can" that 'many widows experience enormously increased sexual arousal immediately after bereavement because the sexual urge is one of the basic primitive urges . . . and in moments of stress or fear or isolation, a sudden overwhelming surge of sexuality can occur'. (David Reuben. Any Woman Can 1976)

Sociologist Helena Lopata, in a study of widowhood in America (1996), correlated fear of sexuality in widowhood with other variables. She found in a questionnaire study that widows who feel isolated tend to see sexual advances in the approaches of other women's husbands, whereas those who do not feel socially so isolated do not. This appears to imply a degree of wish fulfilment or, alternatively, paranoia on the part of lonely widows.

There appears to be some consensus of opinion amongst widows that there is a general loss of interest in sex for about two years after bereavement. This coincides with the most generally quoted period of two years for grieving to take its course after the loss of a spouse. However, there is nothing to suggest that these periods are in any way 'normal'. It is widely accepted that grief and sexuality vary enormously between individuals. Two years is simply a commonly reported period amongst widows themselves for both loss of sexual interest and grieving.

Reports on sexual experiences of widows in the literature to date are mainly anecdotal. Personally, I conformed to both these reported patterns. I experienced an overwhelming urge for sex in the immediate weeks following my husband's death. Once this passed, I did not think about sex again for a couple of years and then it was more because of the sexual advances I began to encounter from others, rather than any inner stirrings. When I did eventually begin to take an interest in sex again, it was more to reaffirm that I was still alive, a real person worthy of full membership in the human race. I didn't really want the sex, not the way I eventually encountered it, with a married man, sneaking it in when opportunity, rather than desire, dictated. But I decided to take it just the same to stay alive, to stay awake and to stay involved with society - even to be a bad member of society seemed preferable to not being one at all. I had a compulsion to tell my married friends that I was having an affair so that they would know that I was no longer a celibate, a maiden aunt, on the shelf, but just like them. And above all, if an attractive man could still want me, that gave my damaged self-image a score of ten thousand in a world in which available women outnumber men by ten to one.

Descriptions by widows in widow-to-widow sessions of their sexual encounters, reveal a variety of motives other than the warmth of human intimacy. I have heard a widow describe the retribution that she felt, against the wives that had slept with her husband, in now sleeping with other women's husbands. For her, sex in widowhood was a weapon. Another described how sex was her defence against rejection and marginalisation. She had found that by sleeping with someone she could gain re-admittance into couple society.

Fidelity in marriage is another factor which may affect sexuality in widowhood. Few today will have been faithful to their husbands all their married lives since 70% of married women report having had extra-marital affairs after five years of marriage (Hite, 1987). Whether women who have come to widowhood from faithful marriages have more or less problems in adjusting to new sexual relationships in widowhood still needs researching.

A paradox emerges from the Hite Report's findings on the attitudes of women to adultery. Of the 70 per cent of married women who reported having had extra-marital affairs after five years of marriage, 87 per cent said that they believed that their husbands were faithful to them, but 79 per cent of these same women said that they themselves had had affairs with married men. These contradictory statistics support the increasingly frequent emergence, after the death of a husband, of other women who had had sexual relationships with him, usually unbeknown to his wife. Nor is this surprising, given the increasing strains on monogamous marriages due to the increasing surplus of women and dearth of available men.

Once one of the members of a widow-to-widow group finds the courage to talk about her husband's infidelity, others usually follow. In the experiences related below, all names have been changed to ensure anonymity.

Judith, a 62-year-old journalist, had known during her marriage that her husband had had an ongoing steady relationship with another woman for some years. There had been an unspoken agreement that as long as this did not interfere with their marriage, it was an acceptable arrangement. She had always felt that she was the 'real' wife legally and psychologically and that the other woman was a dispensable adjunct to the marriage who would be abandoned if anything should happen to upset this. After the husband died, the other woman came out of the closet to attend the funeral. Then she made a claim on the estate on the grounds that she had had a de facto marriage and that the man had promised to leave her money in his Will. The legal wife contested the claim and won the case.

Elizabeth had had a rocky marriage; both she and her husband had had a series of extra-marital affairs and their marriage was in imminent danger of breaking up when he died suddenly of a heart attack. Elizabeth, aged 42, was left with three young children to raise. On sorting through her late husband's possessions she found a letter dated the day he died, in which his current lover had insisted that their affair was over, this time for good. Obsessed by the possibility that this had caused the heart attack, the young widow insisted on meeting the woman. Plagued by guilt, the woman needed to vindicate herself and in so doing revealed to Elizabeth a long-standing serious relationship with her husband, which she had many times sought to put an end to, but which he was unable to break. The two women found a new friendship through their shared problems with the same man.

Jill, a woman I had known for years, had no inkling of her husband's peccadilloes until the day after he died. She was then informed by a friend of an affair he had had with her closest friend some years before. She confronted the friend, who reassured her that 'the affair' had meant nothing - a bit of fun when Jill had been away on holiday one year. She accepted the reassurance, feeling in some way that her friend's shared intimacy with her husband now brought them closer together. The friendship survived.

But, as Jill recovered from the first aftershocks of her husband's death, she began to probe incidents in her past life which would otherwise have gone unnoticed or more accurately, not understood. It began to dawn on her that if the husband she had always believed to be faithful could have betrayed her once 'for a bit of fun' with her best friend, then there was no real reason to doubt that he had done it twice or three times - any number of times in fact. One by one, their past lives began to play themselves out in her mind like a video tape playing backwards. Little, inexplicable incidents popped up in her mind, now demanding explanation. Then she started to hunt for clues in his papers. She found them there - hidden in cryptic telephone number entries and satirical poems. For months she was gripped with a terrible anger which in some ways helped her deal with her grief more effectively. And even worse than the anger was the frustration of never being able to start ,let alone finish, this unfinished business with her husband. Eventually she came to terms with him, perhaps better posthumously than she might have had he been alive. She realised that he must have really loved her, since he had stuck by her through some alluring temptations. What was harder to understand was the need of others to let her know only after her husband had died. It was as though the rules were changed for widows - they being outside the boundaries of civil society , 'an underground current . . . swirling beneath the surface of society', 'a forgotten regiment of women' 'a rising population of outcasts'. (See page 110)

The experience of Joanna, a 61 year old second-language tutor, illustrates how difficult it is for widows to establish a new intimate heterosexual relationship . Widowed at 58, she had decided that she was too young to forego sex for the rest of her life. A couple of years after her husband's death, she set about actively seeking a new partner. But after a couple of abortive attempts to establish a satisfying relationship with a man, she recognised a pattern in the problems she was encountering. She would enter a relationship with the understanding that any new friendship needs a little time to develop the genuine feelings of intimacy which she needed before entering into a sexual relationship. But she soon found that this was impossible. Before any friendship with the men she was encountering could blossom into anything more, they were being snapped up by other women willing to begin a physical relationship immediately. To get a partner in this male deficient widows' world you obviously must be quick off the mark. Joanna's personal sincerity was a handicap to finding a new partner in such a competitive field. She decided to abandon the search , rather than compromise her true feelings and settled instead for more meaningful and honest platonic relationships with the opposite sex.

Lesbianism

Difficult as it is for a person of my generation to accept and not forgetting the religious injunctions against homosexuality of many religions, nevertheless lesbianism is the most logical answer to the sexual needs of the majority of widows. Furthermore, it appears that the next generation of widows will accept homosexuality in its stride. Commenting on a young student's term paper entitled "Intimacy in the Later Years", Betty Friedan reports:

'My student concluded sadly that to those actual older people she interviewed, most of the alternatives for intimate sexual relationships were not acceptable alternatives such as older women dating younger men and lesbians, because these people were raised in stricter period of time when sex was to be had only in traditional marriage' Betty Friedan, **The Fountain of Age** (1994)

The inference is that the student herself, when widowed, will have no problem in accepting lesbianism as a solution to lack of male partners. Incidentally, women of my generation, the generation of these older interviewees, considered themselves to be the ground breakers in sexual liberation and were raised in a period when sex was far from restricted only to traditional marriage, but nevertheless not yet accepting of homosexuality.

Male and female homosexuality has recently been rendered socially acceptable in most Western countries. In the last few years, homosexual couples have appeared in sitcoms that even children view without embarrassment or objection from many a parent. In 'Water Rats', a popular Australian program, Sergeant Helen Blackmore, a successful, vibrant, respected person in society, a police-officer no less, is a lesbian whose passionate sexual relationship with another woman is given full frontal display in a family drama series on prime-time television. And the social acceptance of lesbianism may well affect the behaviour of women who cannot find male sexual partners due to the scarcity of men in present day society. In 'Water Rats', one of the forty-something characters says to another of her own generation 'Everyone knows that women in their thirties and forties experiment with lesbianism today'. Even if everyone doesn't know this, everyone will soon believe it once it has been heard by a few million people on a prime-time television drama.

Masturbation

Germaine Greer outlines the post-modern attitude to genital sex as follows: sex in the late twentieth century is no longer only good for you, but a prerequisite for good health. Muscle contractions during orgasm promote a healthy vagina and doing without sex could lead to a sick one. 'Ergo, if you haven't got a partner you have to have sex with yourself'. Germaine Greer, **The Whole Woman,** (1999)

But for the present generation of widows over 60, masturbation as an outlet for sexual deprivation is also still a problem. While not as taboo as homosexuality in their youth, it was nevertheless still a sin. Children were punished for masturbating and frightened out of their wits by threats of what might happen to them for indulging in this forbidden impulse. They were told that they might be struck deaf or dumb or stutter, rendered sterile or damned to burn eternally in hell.

With modern understanding of sexual gratification in terms of hormonal levels and as a necessity for physical and psychological health, masturbation as a release for sexual tension is now becoming accepted as a convenient strategy, much the same as vitamin tablets are prescribed to complement fast foods. In the United States today, there are centres teaching women, predominantly widows, how to masturbate. The possibility of self-administered sex using direct electrical stimulation of brain cells and promising even more gratifying orgasms than the real thing is already being predicted by some physiologists; and virtual sex is the latest innovation, whereby two human beings bring each other to orgasm via visual and auditory stimulation on the internet.

Not all of us are that liberated but information for self-help is now abundant and accessible through books, magazines and the Internet. Nonetheless, many widows simply suppress their sexuality because they feel that there is no other way of dealing with it. As one widow put it recently 'I don't think it [sex] becomes less important but I think you make it become so because that's the [only] way you have of dealing with it'. **Stanton** (1999),

Intimacy

Of even greater concern to most widows than the loss of sex is the lost physical and psychological intimacy (Lopata, 1979).

When my husband was in the terminal stages of cancer and we knew our time together was fast running out, I said to him one night as we lay side by side in each others arms, that this was what I was going to miss most after he died. And this did indeed prove to be so.

As with sex, loss of intimacy will depend on the amount of intimacy that existed in the marriage. The amount that couples touch each other or stroke each other verbally obviously varies enormously and the deprivation of intimacy and touch will vary accordingly. To some extent the loss of the husband as confidante can be replaced with closer and more meaningful friendships and many widows I know have done so. Women often have intimate non-sexual friendships outside the marriage when their husbands are still alive and these can be strengthened to compensate for the loss when he dies. From my personal experience, new ties can also be formed with other widows, not only because they have the same need for intimacy, but because they are sharing a profound new experience.

Touch hunger

The loss of physical intimacy is more difficult to deal with. In my own experience, I gradually became aware of the problem only several months after my husband's death. There was a build-up with time of what Betty Friedan (one of the leaders of the Women's Liberation Movement in the 60's) refers to as 'touch hunger'.

The sources of human touching outside marriage, of which the widow in her former life was probably never even aware, now begin to assume importance - cuddling and kissing babies or grandchildren, holding hands, linking arms, fondling pets, touching by hairdressers, beauticians, masseurs, manicurists, podiatrists, doctors, even being squeezed in a crowded elevator or bus. These become the only legitimate sources of physical contact and these too might invoke disapproval and guilt if recognised as a means of allaying 'touch hunger'. I shudder to think how these notions might translate into the already abundant demonology of widowhood.

Just as friendships can be strengthened to replace the lost spouse as a confidante, so too can physical intimacy be increased. I found quite unconsciously that I was holding hands with friends, especially close girlfriends, something I had never done before. One day when something upset me rather badly, I remember pacing around the house about to burst into tears when the idea suddenly struck me to hop in the car and drive to my best friend's house. 'I need a hug', I blurted at her as she opened the front door and, without saying a word, she held me tight until I said 'O.K.'. Since then I haven't even needed to say what I need - she has learned to read my face just as my husband once did.

. I remember David saying to me years ago, 'In the end we are all alone'. But widowhood has taught me that before the end, none of us should be alone. I realise now that I should have had a network of intimate relationships before David died.

To become equipped to deal with the realities of modern widowhood, we will first have to recognise that widowhood has now become a significant phase of the human life cycle requiring proactive planning is much as any of the other discrete phases in our lives.

CHAPTER 10

Widow power

O n becoming a widow, I discovered that the Women's Movement had forgotten me. So amazed was I at this apparent oversight that I embarked upon a search for references to widowhood in all the major landmark books of the Women's Movement. I drew a blank on serious treatment of this subject in all of them. I could not believe my own discovery. How could such an array of brilliant women, the world's greatest proponents of women' issues, have avoided widowhood Ten per cent of the women that this movement represents are widowed, yet none of its leaders or writers were sufficiently motivated by their plight.to include them in their crusades for women's rights.

Widows have inherited the legacy of centuries of discrimination and denial inflicted upon them, so that today they do not recognize their own right to representation alongside their single, married, divorced and lesbian sisters. The exclusion of widowhood from modern politics cannot simply be attributed to our lingering patriarchal tradition. I have found that hostile opposition to some of the claims in this book have come only from women. I have not encountered hostility from a single man - incredulity sometimes, but never hostility. It is interesting that Jessica Bernard in her study of marriage observed the same phenomenon. 'Women', she wrote, 'are even more prejudiced [against women] than men'! Bernard J. (1972)

Women do not like to think about widowhood and widows do not like to live it. Many widows simply want to escape it, either by trying to 'get' a man to relegitimise their position in society or, failing this, to hide their status by keeping a low profile. As mentioned earlier, many widows are loath to join widow support groups, or to socialise with other widows, or even with exclusively women groups because people will think they are all widowed. The only way that Greer Fay Cashman (social corresponded for the Jerusalem Post) and I were able to start a widows' support group in Jerusalem was by disguising our intention. Our first advertisement in The Jerusalem Post calling for widows interested in forming a social support group drew a blank. Re-wording the advertisement to make it appear that we were embarking on a research project drew an overwhelming response. In the rap sessions that followed, the widows said again and again that they had not responded to the first advertisement because they did not like to be seen socialising with other widows; they felt demeaned by that identity.

Even Lynne Caine (1974), in one of the most sensitive accounts of modern widowhood to date, wrote 'and so the widow is left . . . in that ghetto of unwanted lonely women, the one that I recoiled from so abruptly when I realised how easy it was to sink into that world apart . . .'

Caine said she wrote 'Widow' to share her experiences and feelings in the hope that this would 'help other widows survive as persons, knowing who they are, instead of slamming head-on into an identity crisis'. But in the end Caine's only solution was to escape; firstly, to escape the company of other widows and finally to escape from widowhood itself by remarrying - a solution not possible for most widows. She saw widowhood as an obstacle to be avoided, an impediment to be overcome.

Perhaps it was not yet possible in her time to view widowhood as a challenge to grow and for which to fight for society's recognition. But just about a decade later, another widow decided to stand her ground and challenge society, rather than escape or hide from it. In an essay published in the New York Times, journalist Genevieve Davis Ginsberg wrote:

'I was dragged by my heels into this so-called passage, but now that I'm here I've come to appreciate the opportunity to find a person buried under so many layers of daughter, wife, mother . . . I was searching for acknowledgment of widowhood as a bona fide life stage . . . a stage where the quest is not limited to replacing one partner with another or remaining a wife without a husband for the rest of my life.'. And she concluded '**widowhood needs to be re-invented both for those who live it and those who fear it**'. Ginsberg, (1987)

In The Fountain of Age, Betty Friedan (1993) predicted that it would require 'a political movement to effect the changes necessary for society to use productively the wisdom and generativity of age because she claimed the aged were still stereotyped as infantile and feeble in spite of modern research evidence to the contrary.

The challenge for widows is even stronger because in addition to the prejudices against age. they are also burdened with the mythology and taboos of sex and death. Widows too will need a political movement to achieve acceptance and productive integration into society. The time is ripe for widows to take responsibility for themselves. Never has widowhood been so clearly defined as it is today as a significant and prolonged phase of women's lives. Widows could now become a powerful minority, but to achieve this, widows will have to overcome their own lowered self-esteem, come out of the closet and make themselves heard.

Today the main activities offered to older women, mainly widows, are those vacated by younger married women who have since won the right to work at real jobs. Legitimate places for wives to while away their leisure time before the present acceptance of the working wife and mother were in church clubs or as volunteers for a large variety of charitable organisations and as museum guides. Now these are largely the sanctuaries for lonely widows futilely seeking meaningful ways to reconnect with life.

But these activities never did anything to advance the causes of women or wives . It was the consciousness raising crusades of the Women's Liberation Movement that swept across the USA in the 60s and finally the whole Western world in the in the 70s, that did. And now it can only be consciousness raising in the widow-to-widow groups which will advance the status of widows. Widows must set about improving their lot with a political lobby. To begin with, they should take the care of widows out of the hands of counsellors and psychiatrists. They could lobby for funds to research the problems of widowhood and to subsidise projects which would result from such research for the promotion of health and psychological growth of widows and to expand the scope and activities of widow-to-widow support groups. A widows' lobby should also campaign for special training programs to enable widows to find useful and rewarding work because widows need to work for psychological and social reasons peculiar to their situation. Employment programs for widows would cut social welfare and health insurance costs, possibly sufficiently to fund the programs themselves. Widowed women are on the whole mature, healthy people suddenly freed of former responsibilities. If forced into isolation and idleness by society, it is predictable that they will become old and ill before their time and a drain on the welfare funds of society. Available roles for widows would re-open the channels back to society. Social and economic self-reliance will in turn help to remove the social stigma and self-denigration of widowhood.

Housing for widows is one of most important areas in need of research. A lobby for widows could advocate a commission to study specific alternatives for housing for widows, to alleviate the crushing psychological effects on many of being forced to live alone, often for the first time in their lives. Or for those who prefer to live alone, to reduce their vulnerability to violence and robbery or medical emergency, etc. There is already a growing industry of senior citizen housing alternatives, but the needs of the widowed must be recognised as a unique category, separate from age. The needs of the elderly do not always encompass the needs of the widow (and widows are not always old.). Housing in widowhood is a complex subject which will produce many alternatives, all better than today's wasteful, unhappy spectacle of one widow per isolated family cottage rattling aimlessly around her six or seven empty rooms of memories, as is happening in many of the older suburbs in urban areas everywhere in the Western world.

It might be argued that the political representation of widows would promote their continuing identification as dead men's wives, thus hampering them from becoming women in their own right. But it is not widowhood that prevents a widow from becoming her own person again, but society's discrimination against her. This will never be altered by denying it.

It might also be argued that because widows are not only widows but also doctors and lawyers, shop assistants and secretaries, mothers and granmothers, etc., their political representation would be inappropriate. But widows do share two important common denominators – their marginalisation by society and their potential political strength in numbers to promote their own interests. These two alone should be worthy of any widow's vote. *Widows are probably the only identifiable adult group left that has not come out on its own behalf to demand an end to discrimination and its inalienable right to the pursuit of happiness.*

How long now before we see the first candidate standing for election to parliament on a widows' ticket with 10 per cent of the voting female population to back her!

CHAPTER 11

Widowhood in the 21st Century

The Widow Wave

Because of the extended years of life expectancy and the arrival of the baby-boom generation at the beginning of old age there is at present an obsession with the economic threat that aging populations of the post-industrial countries are posing to the young. This approaching age-wave will consist largely of women, mostly widowed and still no-one is addressing their specific needs or assessing their potential!

Failure to recognise that the age problem is significantly a widow problem will lead to inefficient and even counter-productive planning.

While the problems of age are now being widely studied, those of widowhood have hardly been acknowledged. The body of professionals - gerontologists, psychologists, psychiatrists, sociologists - currently gearing up to tackle the approaching tidal wave of senior citizens is steadfastly ignoring the large scale, long-term widowhood which a large proportion of these senior citizens will experience.

Treating males and females as a unit in the study of aging is comparable to lumping males and females together in studies on breast cancer. In both cases the individuals involved are over-whelmingly female. In the past the majority of older people who lived alone in the West were widows. In 1996, almost 700 000 men and women in Australia lived alone and 480 000 of these, i.e. almost 70 per cent, were widows (ABS, 1996). The number of single households has grown exponentially since 1996 and by 2006 there were more than 2 million single household i.e.24% of all households .

It is now predicted that by 2026 single person households will outnumber nuclear families. The subject of single households in the past was overwhelmingly a widow, based phenomenon and should have been addressed as such . But this was not recognised and consequently there are no studies available to date on the housing problems of widowhood.

Housing for single occupancy has now transitioned into a much broader based phenomenon which will need to be studied from several different separate population interests: by age, single parents and divorcees, apart from widows and widowers.

There are fundamental differences between the elderly who are married and the elderly who are widowed. One is the most obvious and terrible problem of loneliness. Another is their relative economic situations. Couples who live on the age pension allowances are better off than single elderly people because the cost of living for a couple is not twice that of a single. A study carried out in 1997 by the University of New South Wales found that a single older person living on a government pension spends 30 per cent less than a married couple living at the same standard, but receives approximately 40 per cent less in pension allowance.

In 'The Age Wave', a landmark book on the aging society of Western civilisation, widowhood gets just two entries in the index, in one of which the author, Ken Dichtwald, despairs over the fact that 'there are now five times as many widows as widowers and fully half of all women over 65 are widows. 'How will the emotional needs of the single older women be met?', he asks and leaves it at that, in a book whose purpose is to plan for the changing demographic, social and economic consequences of an aging society.

Age and widowhood

While the problems of age and widowhood are often interchangeable or complementary because of the extensive overlap of the populations they embrace (ie. the elderly are commonly widowed and widows are usually elderly), there is nevertheless a vast difference in the experience of aging as a married woman or as a widow. The older married woman still has the status of a protected female even if her husband is sick and ailing, senile or demented. When my own husband was in the terminal stage of cancer, I still did not experience the loss in status and rejection by society that were to assail me after he died. And I recall now that I did not see my own mother as vulnerable and unprotected until the day she became a widow, although she was already in her mid-seventies and quite frail and my father had been in a nursing home for a whole year before he died. Widowhood is blighted by a stereotype of its own apart from that of ageism and as widows are usually older women most widows are afflicted by the prejudices against both widowhood and age.

Because we are the first generation to experience these extended years of widowhood, we have no role models and so we tend erroneously to hold on to old inappropriate stereotypes and prejudices. Even the concept of age itself is now distorted. What was formerly considered old is now no longer 'old' but middle-aged since life spans have extended

Widowhood has similarly changed dramatically in the last half-century. Widows today are better educated, freer of the responsibility for dependent children, more economically independent, healthier and with more years of widowhood ahead of them than ever before in history. But the old image of widows as vulnerable, frail, dependent, poor, incompetent women persists both in society in general and amongst widows themselves.

As the attack on the mythologies of age progresses, the stereotypes of the elderly are crumbling and older people look, dress, think, feel and behave differently today than a generation ago. As women, widows too look and behave differently from women a generation ago, but as widows they are still reporting the same old feelings of inferiority, denigration, dependency, vulnerability, loss of status, rejection, lack of purpose, marginalisation as their surviving mothers and even grand-mothers(there are now increasing instances of 3 generations of surviving widows in one family) With this image of themselves, widows think and act from a position of weakness when the facts should place them in a position of strength.

Betty Friedan, in the <u>Fountain of Age</u>, questions how much of what the elderly experience in growing old is real and how much is due to society stereotyping them and their own assimilation of those stereotyped views New research is revealing new kinds of cognitive capacities that develop with age, yet mental decline with age is still taken for granted by most people and the elderly are still progressively treated more like children than adults as they age.

Similarly, widows are lumbered with the persistence of archaic views of widowhood. Like the elderly, widows are better off economically than they were. The poorer amongst them have better pension provisions, like the aged. The less poor, too, are wealthier than ever before with full inheritance rights to their husbands' estates.

Stereotypes not only influence the view other people have of the target population. Even more damaging to those targeted is the effect stereotyping has on their own self-image. Because of the current rapid ageing of Western populations, efforts are increasing to dislodge the old stereotypes of age and, older people today see themselves differently from a generation ago. But even though the majority of widows are older women and their own self-image as older women has changed, their perception of themselves as *widows* has not.

I have learnt from first-hand experience that my own initial psychological reaction to widowhood widowhood - (the loss of status, feelings of shame and alienation, self-pity, vulnerability, incompetence, dependency, sexual ambiguity, delegitimisation, second-class citizenship, of being a threat, of having exited the mainstream of human society) - was overwhelmingly due to society's view of widows and my own assimilation of these views.

Within a few months of my husband's death, I was successfully running our business affairs; within a year I had become a self-sufficient adult for the first time in my life. I had shed what is called by June Singer, the Jungian psychologist, 'the ungratified baby rewards of marriage' - the unresolved dependencies of childhood for which my husband had replaced my parents as provider and protector. Within two years, I had overcome the grief and learnt to live serenely with the pain of an irreplaceable loss. But I am still grappling with society's prejudices, fears and denial of widowhood and may be for the rest of my life unless they change.

There is a crucial difference between society's image of old people and 'us' (old people) as we know ourselves to be. A nationwide study in the United States to determine popular images of aging revealed that a majority of Americans saw old people as not very physically active, not very sexually active, not very openminded and not very useful to society (Friedan, 1997).

Because studies of the elderly were, in the past, carried out mainly by the non-elderly, the wrong problems have been studied. Younger people studying older people speak of their subjects as 'them' (not 'us') and have been unable to identify many of the questions crucial to older people. Studies have consequently focused on the *weaknesses* of age, e.g. osteoporosis, dependency on social welfare systems, dementia etc., instead of the *strengths* that enable men and women to live so much longer than before. There is a lesson in this for the future study of widowhood. Widowhood, like age, is today an inevitable part of the human life cycle. Those who would study widowhood, like age, must be able to accept that widows are *us - not them.*

Widowhood is an intensely subjective experience and it is therefore important that widowhood also be studied by widows themselves. In a radio interview on Australian national radio with Helena Lopata, Susan Feldman stated that 'most widows are happy'. Helena Lopata was a pioneer of scientific research into widowhood, breaking new ground with her studies of widows in Chicago in the 1970s. Susan Feldman was at that time engaged in a doctoral research project on widowhood in Melbourne. But neither Helena Lopata nor Susan Feldman were widows. I have never met a widow who would make the blanket statement 'widows are happy' or allow it to pass without comment.

Similarly, Desmond Morris (The Human Sexes, 1997) states categorically that 'in contrast to Islamic cultures where unattached females can only be whores, adulteresses or pathetic loners, in the West most of the surplus females . . . become career- women. ... lesbians . . . or, if they do live alone, enjoy an active outgoing social life'. Certainly, many more unattached females are likely to become career women and lesbians than attached ones, but widows, the majority of whom live alone, certainly do not enjoy active outgoing social lives (Helena Lopata, 1987).

Redefining widow

'Widow is a harsh and hurtful word...I resent what it has come to mean' *(Caine, 1974).*

Millions of widows resent the widow word. While Mrs (or Ms) is a title of respect, 'widow' is a label of despair. Layer after layer of innuendo has attached to the term widow. But even before its inception into European languages, it brought with it a 'harsh and hurtful' message from its root in Latin.

Sylvia Plath superbly captured the putrefying damnation embedded in the 'widow.' word:

Widow. The word consumes itself...

Widow. The dead syllable...

Widow. The bitter spider sits and sits in the centre of her loveless spokes...

Widow. That great, vacant estate...

'Because women broke through the feminine mystique and redefined themselves in terms no longer limited to their biological sex role . they could deal with the traumas of menopause' (Friedan, 1997). Similarly, only after women have broken through the widowhood mystique and redefined themselves in terms no longer limited to the role (or rather non-role) of defunct wife, will they be able to deal with the traumas of widowhood.

The first step will be to eliminate the negativity from the concept of widow. According to the Oxford Dictionary, a widow is presently:

'a woman whose husband has died'

i.e., a woman who either was married and no longer is, (negative)

or a woman who is married to a man who no longer exists (negative).

To turn this definition into a positive, one could redefine widow as:

'a woman who has survived her husband'

'a woman who was formerly married and is now in the post-marital phase of life'

Gail Sheehy writes, 'menopause causes women to panic and question 'Won't I ever be me anymore?' But Betty Friedan asserts that 'the overwhelming evidence . . . indicates that, in vital age (that is, successful age), women as well as men become more and more themselves'. Similarly, to successfully negotiate widowhood, the widow who is today an ambiguous non-person must be replaced by the woman who in widowhood becomes more and more her own person. A widow should not be defined in terms of who she *was*, but who she now *is*. A widow should not be seen as a woman whose husband has died but as a woman who is nobody's anything but her own person. The negativity in the label 'widow' is impeding widows from finding this person.

Men who survive their wives don't have a problem with the word 'widower'. Whether the widower is a dead woman's husband is a non-issue, because the widower is never identified as a dead woman's husband. In fact, the word 'widower' is rarely even used in any context, . A survey of British newspapers for the year 2011, comparing the ratio of the use of the word widow to widower reported 475 to 50 in the Guardian, 729 to 14 in the Daily

Mail, 918 to 147 in the Sun (Matt Mills, the Guardian 16/4/12). (demographically the ratio of widows to widowers is 5 to 1!)

Widows are commonly identified as widows where their marital status is irrelevant. For example, headlines such as 'Widow awaiting cancer surgery 'In the Daily Mail, or "Widow must re-home 13 cats or face 20,000 pound fine... In other words, in the collective psyche widows remain *dead men's wives* for the rest of their lives. But widowers are never identified as dead women's husbands.

There is also a problem arising out of the origin of the widow word itself. The root of the word widow comes from the Latin 'viduus' meaning empty, void. Sylvia Plath captured the legacy of this connection with the Latin root in one mighty line of poetry;

'Widow: that great vacant (empty) estate'!

The Hebrew Bible also echoes this meaning in Ruth's lament
, 'Filled I departed . . . Yahweh brings me back empty' (Ruth 1:21).

The underlying implication of the widow word ever since its inception has been negative - one of irreparable loss, diminution, deprivation. It is time to find an alternative. Just as spinsters became singles, Negroes became Blacks, unmarried mothers became single parents, old people became senior citizens, so too now should the widow word be recognised for what it is and discarded.

One suggestion could be marital survivor, a title of honour and achievement instead of loss and shame. Another could be to follow the life passages, single, married, independent senior or single senior.

Shakespeare, in Romeo and Juliet, asked rhetorically:
"what's in a name?" And he answered "a rose by any other name would smell the same" (or words to that effect).

That may be so, for roses but not for widows for whom, like the spinsters, Negroes and single mothers of yesteryear, it would seem there is indeed much in a name!

CHAPTER 12

Whither Widowhood

Today, 80% of all widowed persons are female (Table 3 Appendix) and, with the continuing aging of the population in Western societies, the number of widows and the proportion of women to men widowed, is going to continue to increase at least for the next 20 years, until the baby boom generation has completed its widowhood years. This adds up to one enormous growing demographic social problem.

The need for an intimate adult relationship is deeply ingrained and extremely strong. Whether this is a biological need or conditioned by a prolonged intimate union with a spouse, or a combination of both is irrelevant to the 80% of present generation of widows who will never re-partner.

Widows today who are realistic no longer assess remarriage as a viable option and direct their energies in other directions to reformulate their lives. Many seek. entry into the workforce, often for the first time. New careers are difficult ambitions late in life, but nevertheless sought after and attained by considerable numbers of widows. I have met widows who in their sixties and even early seventies have retrained for new careers - aromatherapy massage, reflexology, the Rabbinate, locality arbitrators, master chefs and Peace Corps volunteers. Many seek further education simply for the love of learning and the excitement of opening new horizons with the time, resources and freedom they have to indulge themselves often for the first time.

Some physically relocate again to the campuses of their youth to find new communities to share this new phase in life with. In these new living arrangements, communities of older people, largely widows, are forming self-sufficient societies in which individuals can find satisfying new roles, rewarding work in groundbreaking new social experiments for caring and cooperative rather than competitive ways of living.

The concept of human intimacy and sexual fulfilment in an adult one-to-one relationship is still central to our culture and most modern widows would still, I believe, confirm that their marriages were worth the heavy price that widowhood exacts. Marriage remains a sacred cow that thirty years of intensive consciousness raising by the Women's Liberation Movement has not displaced. The overwhelming evidence is that marrying (at least once) will remain one of most women's goals, if not any longer the only one.

If marriage is to remain a central part of human socialisation, then so too is widowhood. What we should be aiming at is to modify marriage to better suit the conditions of our times. More emphasis must be placed on the strains and stresses that marriage in its present form is placing on the individuals who partake of it, not least of which are the extensive years of widowhood that can be expected to follow it.

Marriage in the post- industrial world is no longer solely, or even primarily, concerned with the promotion of child rearing. While still intricately connected with reproduction and child rearing, it is now even more involved with the needs of adults. For the first time in history, the focus of marriage has shifted from child rearing, which is taking place more and more outside of marriage, to the emotional needs of adults.

Like 'the new third age', the substantial and growing population of older widows is a new phenomenon in human history. And
widowhood, again like age itself, may be capable of triggering a
new potential for growth and creativity. But this potential is being
frustrated by misconceptions and prejudices which view widowhood as a misfortune.

Widows as an effective force in society will be a new phenomenon. How will this new cohesive population of mature women,
empowered with longest life expectations in human history, liberated from former responsibilities to others and with substantial
economic independence, find its role? What can it contribute to
the enrichment of our aging society in which it occupies a core
position? How will it navigate the uncharted territory of a world
of unprecedented distortion of gender ratios?

We are the pioneering generation in prolonged widowhood,
breaking new ground and groping in the dark to find solutions to
often overwhelming problems. Those following behind us should
have an easier time in widowhood; with the advancement of
women to full and equal legal and economic power, the erosion of
the importance of marriage in defining women's worth and, above
all, their equal participation in the work force

It will be up to widows themselves to claim their right to full
participation on the centre stage of life, to find new ways to move
in society, to make it happen for them.

Appendix I: Proposed areas for the study of widowhood

Studies of widowhood should of course include positive aspects as well as negative ones. There has been unrelenting resistance in the past to see anything positive in widowhood, because what little attention this subject has to date received has been mainly from male doctors and psychiatrists treating widows as patients for 'excessive' grieving and depression (Lieberman, 1966). Anything positive in widowhood will imply that women can manage without male protection and this can be enormously threatening to some men. And even among widows themselves, there has been a resistance to see anything positive in widowhood.

Pro-active planning

Two gerontologists, Eva and Boaz Kahana, noted strong 'resemblances between their hardy fellow survivors of the Holocaust and older people who chose to leave their homes and roots to strike out for new lives . . . In both instances, the previous roles that defined one's humanness were stripped away . . . Both groups were remarkably pro-active, recognising that they could not just follow old routines as if life could go on as before; They recognised that they had to change tasks and ties, to find new sources of purpose'. Widowhood, which even more than age strips us of 'previous roles', can be expected to bear similar resemblances to pro-active behaviour in successful survivors.

Controlled studies are needed to verify and expand on this speculation - does pro-active behaviour benefit all widows, or only some, in successfully negotiating widowhood? Are those widows who succeed in re-establishing heterosexual partnerships or re-marrying, more or less successful in managing their lives after widowhood than those who establish new ways of living rather than seeking to replace what was lost with more of the same?

Important practical guidelines would emerge from such studies. Should widows in general be encouraged to leave their familiar surroundings, resist the impulse to find new partners or to increase family ties with children and siblings and move on to new experiences? Would this be good for some and bad for others and if so whom? And if good for some, how soon after bereavement? In general studies should be undertaken to locate the major differences in experience and attitudes between widows who have been eminently successful in negotiating the transition to widowhood and those who have failed badly.

With the ageing of our society, some innovative pro-active individuals are now beginning to face the unfaceable and plan for the future ahead of widowhood. In an article entitled 'Age of Consent' which appeared in the Vogue Australia issue of September 1996, Jill Spalding outlined a project she had initiated to enlist a group of friends to plan for their old age together. 'Over a series of lunches [they] formulated a working plan: a condominium with separate living areas, but shared library, dining areas, etc...[situated in] a lively cultural community . . .'. They enlisted a lawyer to oversee the technicalities of collecting funds to be put into escrow to buy the premises, which would be rented out until the first of the group needed to move in. The group elected members from amongst themselves to handle accountancy, domestic scheduling, etc. The eligibility for entry was turning eighty (such is the confidence amongst young Australian women today of reaching this age). Interestingly, the 'project' only included women, although no specific mention of this fact appears anywhere in the article. So in reality, it was overwhelmingly a project for widowhood as 65 per cent of Australian women over the age of eighty in 1996 were widows, compared with 8 per cent never married singles, 23 per cent still married and 3 per cent divorcees (ABS, 1996) and the proportion widowed will increase still further before Jill Spalding reaches eighty.

The success of such pro-active planning will only be ascertainable in the future when enough time has elapsed to follow a generation of women which has lived through the reality.

Involvement in the world outside the home

What are the effects on widowhood for women who have dropped out of the workforce to rear children? Even if women don't give up their jobs completely but resort instead to part-time employment, they lose their edge in the competitive job market and much of their community network during the years of early motherhood. This is likely to have profound consequences for them in the later years of life and especially in widowhood. We need hard data to enable women to make informed decisions about the social and psychological costs in widowhood of dropping out of the workforce, because these penalties will only be felt years into the future.

The widow-to-widow groups.

More and more alternative treatments such as relaxation exercises, natural products with believed curative powers and massage therapies are being used to treat the aged, in place of expensive high-tech cures such as medication, radiology and chemotherapy.

The major example of a successful low-tech alternative cited by Betty Friedan in the <u>Fountain of Age</u> is the 'widow-to-widow' groups (i.e., widow support groups run by widows themselves). Yet on what authority she claims this is hard to guess since as yet no controlled studies have been carried out to measure the effectiveness of these groups or even their success in attracting widows to join them. Research is urgently needed for the study of such enterprises and how to improve their functioning. For example, by trial and error in my own group founded in Jerusalem in 1995, it was eventually found necessary to form smaller sub-groups to cater for new widows whose immediate need for grief support was not being met in the parent group.

Research is needed to investigate the effect on widows' health of widow-to-widow groups. If the anticipated positive results emerge, public and private health insurance subsidiaries should be available for such enterprises as group therapy and to subsidise the endeavours of such groups in life-enhancing activities. This would be more effective and less toxic and less expensive than presently insured 'medical' treatment for the 'problems' of widowhood resulting from loneliness, lack of intimacy, touch hunger, etc.

Widowhood is still erroneously treated as an abnormality in need of a cure. As long as this attitude persists, money is unlikely to be allocated to research such enterprises as widow-to-widow groups, which could, if Friedan is right, save millions of dollars on aged medical care. Furthermore, official recognition of the value of widow-to-widow groups would help to overcome the present resistance of widows to join these groups because of low self-esteem.

Peer counselling.

To counter the growing isolation of older people, the Senior Health and Peer Counselling Centre in Santa Monica (USA) has trained hundreds of older, non-professional people since 1977 to help their peers through the transition to a new view of aging.

Widows are deeply affected by the isolation resulting from the increasing transience of interpersonal relationships in modern society. A Widowhood Health and Peer Counselling Centre, like the Santa Monica Centre for Seniors, would not only help new widows to a new view of widowhood but at the same time, provide meaningful and relevant work for other widows as volunteer counsellors.

Widow communities.

With the death of a spouse, most widows find themselves suddenly dependent on friends, family and neighbours for company, advice and physical help. To diffuse this dependency and give widows a first stepping stone to self-reliance, well-established support systems should be available in which the new widow could find both initial support and later a role in widow-administered organisations offering a myriad of basic services such as committees for accommodation, meals, household repairs, legal and banking advice, counselling services, etc.

Such support systems need to be specifically for widows - not, as is now the case, just senior citizens. A newly widowed woman sees herself and is seen by others, as different from non-widowed seniors; she needs to have a place where she belongs. Of course, as with widow-to-widow support groups, widows will have first to be freed of their present loss of self-esteem to gain sufficient confidence to proclaim their widowhood publicly and associate openly with other widows. All members of these communities should have to contribute in some way. Here, there will be purpose, role and community at a fraction of the cost of institutionalised care which unfortunately is still the ultimate destiny of so many widows today.

It could be argued that this would create a community apart reinforcing the marginalisation of widows. But widow communities need not isolate widows any more than senior housing-communities isolate seniors. At least there would be an option. Not all widowed women would choose to join such a community, but for those who do there would be a choice, an alternative to living alone. And for those who don't, living alone or with children would then become options of more dignified choice.

Secondly, the communities themselves could and should interact with the larger community - penetrate the pubs and the clubs, the theatres and cinemas, organise bridge and chess teams to compete with other local teams, provide speakers to raise consciousness on widowhood issues to nurses, doctors, accountants, insurance agents, senior couples, high school students, etc. Rather than isolate widows, widow communities would thus enhance their integration in society.

Widownet.

SeniorNet is a well-established internet site. Less well known, however, is Widownet, where hundreds of notices, letters, replies and words of encouragement and advice are exchanged every day.

Widownet could be used, like SeniorNet, to organise lobbying campaigns for specific widow issues such as housing and employment, legal services, finance benefits and a widow lobby.

Housing.

The numbers of people living alone is growing and this growth is in no small measure due to growth in the numbers of older widows living alone, as improving health keeps them progressively longer out of institutionalised care facilities.

New studies reported in the Journal of the American Medical Association found that living alone posed a 'major independent risk factor' for life comparable to physiological factors like heart disease: not divorce, separation, or death of a spouse, but the sheer fact of living alone.

Although loneliness is the most frequently reported problem of widowhood, nevertheless many widows prefer to live alone and retain their independence. But this is often only a choice between the lesser of two evils. Various new experimental housing projects for single people have been attempted in recent years. One such project comprised a community of widows who, previously strangers to each other, moved into a low-cost low-rise Californian apartment block in 1965. After the daughter of one of the residents put a coffee machine in the recreation room, a social interaction began to develop amongst them. As people came downstairs to fetch their mail mid-morning, they looked into the recreation room, found six or seven people drinking coffee and some joined in. From this, a recreation committee developed and half a year later Merrill Court was a beehive of activity - study-groups, visiting groups to hospitals or orphanages, working groups to make things to sell and spend the money on group fun activities etc. 'These activities gave the widows a sense of identity. If one was no longer a mother, wife, provider or earner, one was at least a Birthday Chairman (arranging celebrations as a new career), a Treasurer, a member of the Handicrafts Committee - new roles for anyone who wanted one and with each new role, with each new responsibility, the widows built themselves a new identity' (Hochschild, 1973).

The spatial arrangement of the apartments fostered this enlivening sense of community. The living rooms and porches all faced out on a common outside walkway, so they saw one another coming and going. This led to concern if someone failed to appear for a few days and eventually the widows cared for each other in ill health.

Rivalries and differences developed, but never alienation or isolation. Hochschild calls it a 'peer bond' based on reciprocity, similarity and equality as opposed to parent/child, us/them, equations and the unequal relationship of staff/resident in institutions.

For these widows, their sisterhood developed out of adult autonomy. 'Instead of playing the role of 'old person', they . . . improvised new roles', but at the same time they did not deny the realities of aging. Remarkably, 'none of them fulfilled the age mystique of deterioration and decline into senility before death. Six residents died in the course of (this study) . . . five of the six died in the course of their daily duties. Only one died in hospital after a few days of not feeling well'. It is not unreasonable to propose from this study that the isolation of widows in society is psychological abuse, which inflicts grave mental and physical harm and is probably contributing generously to exploding national health insurance budgets.

I came across a similar accidental arrangement of widows who occupied an entire level of one apartment block in Houston, Texas, thus forming an 'extended family'. When one died, the others requested the inheritors of the apartment to allow them to handle the re-sale to ensure that another widow of their choosing moved in. This commune has now been going for nearly twenty years, with all the pioneers now dead and an entire second generation in occupation.

A new development in the USA is whole communities of older people settling around universities. There is a newly emerging population of elders returning to universities now encouraging them to fill the seats left empty by the decline in undergraduates at the end of the baby-boom cycle. Such a development could be promoted as an alternative communal living style for widows who want options to living alone in widowhood - housing for widows to mirror student accommodation in buildings adapted to their needs in University locations. A UK study has reported that 15 per cent of people over 65 are now studying and that women participate more than men. Since more than 50 per cent of woman over 65 are widowed, widows must be contributing a sizeable proportion of senior students.

Another type of housing arrangement taking root in Los Angeles involves the adaptation of existing accommodation to a shared-housing setup. This may take the form of renting out a room to another widow or to a younger family member, perhaps a college student, or, if finances permit, adding on an apartment or self-contained wing for a tenant or friend. Whether these arrangements involve payment of rent or a barter agreement of help and shared living expenses is immaterial to the basic aim of reducing loneliness and isolation.

The West Hollywood based **Alternative Living for the Aging** operates five co-operative apartment communities for the low-income elderly serving the entire Los Angeles area. It also specialises in matching up suitable people to share their accommodations. Although open to all, the majority of people involved in this project are widows.

In Sydney, Australia, a new scheme was started late last century to register groups of women who live alone with a view to forming housing complexes around common interests. For example, for those interested in art, the complex would have a common studio; for gardeners, it would have a common area to cultivate;

for those wanting to generate income, it would have a child-minding centre. The aim was to create bonds through shared activity, to create interests and to produce income.

Housing is one of the few areas in which a start has been made in addressing the specific needs of widows. No doubt the innovative alternatives will continue to multiply as the number of widows living alone continues to grow. What is urgently needed now is a comparative study of the pros and cons of the various models already in existence to improve future ventures in this field. Creative housing for widows is an attractive potential commercial enterprise which, once recognised, will quickly mushroom and benefit from healthy competition for a growing market. Organisation will lead to lowered costs, with pooled resources for sharing health facilities and services such as catering, laundering, class insurance, equipment hiring, etc. The possibilities for harnessing the potential trade of such a time-rich, experience-rich, property-rich, health-improving, age-extending population now living in lonely disarray are truly mind-boggling

.

Widowhood as business.

There are approximately 35 million widows in the developed countries - enough to justify any commercial attention or political wooing. A welter of industries is now gearing up to meet the needs of ageing populations and the travel industry at least is beginning to show a glimmering of recognition that their target clientele may be widows as well as married elders. Caribbean cruises for seniors now come equipped with sixty-plus-year-old male hosts whose job it is to provide male company for widows on excursions, on the dancefloor, at meals, etc.

One of the big differences for widows as a subgroup of elders is the financial penalty for single occupancy. Ever since Noah's Ark, the travel industry has been double-occupancy oriented.

Travel Companion Exchange Inc. aims to help senior singles get around that penalty by finding a pre-selected compatible companion. But far better would be legislation prohibiting discrimination against singles in charging practices. This should be an issue for a future widows' political platform.

. There are now a welter of institutes for senior education, e.g., the Elderhostel movement established in the USA in 1975 and the University of the Third Age started in the UK; the Institute for Retired Professionals started in New York; the Institute for Learning in Retirement started in Cambridge, Massachusetts; the Senior Studies Institute of Strathclyde, University of Scotland; the Plato Society in Los Angeles. Elderhostel helped start about 36 of these institutes for seniors to continue learning after they've done an initial Elderhostel trip.

Again, as the majority of retirees are eventually widowed women, these enterprises ought to be specifically focusing on the needs of widows in addition to the needs of retirees in general.

Grandparents associations.

In the last few years grand-parents associations have begun to appear.

'Foster Grandparents' in Fort Ord, California, go into homes with problems of child abuse 'as a respected non-threatening presence and help the mothers learn to care for their children without violence'. The foster grandparents are given formal training for this role.

The British Grandparents Federation was set up in 1987 to help grandparents who have the care of young relatives and to speak to groups of social workers, magistrates and other professionals involved with young people. It helps grandparents who may be involved in legal battles for custody or care of grandchildren. It published a newsletter, a pamphlet on the 1989 Children's Act and a collection of stories from grandparents with grandchildren in care. It has played a substantial role in the law governing care rights and is regularly consulted by academics, media and government bodies.

The grandparents who participate in these organisations will be predominantly grandmothers as they outlive the grandfathers four to one. It is interesting to note that one of the theories proffered to explain the fact that women live approximately five years longer than men purely due to genetic advantage, was the added survival value of grandmothers to the species because, even in prehistoric times, they may have remained involved in caring for the grand-children past their own reproductive years (Morris, 1997). The steep rise in the number of working married mothers, of divorce rates and single mothers is now likely to increase the involvement of widows in grandchild rearing. This could become an area of widespread deployment for considerable numbers of widows war-ranting government encouragement and support.

Sexuality.

For older women who, for whatever reason, do retain a need for sex, the problem in widowhood is clear enough. There simply are not enough free older men to partner single older women. The other possibilities are polygyny, younger men as partners, mastur-bation and lesbianism. There is no data available relating to the practice of masturbation or lesbianism amongst widows. Older women marrying or partnering younger men, though still compar-atively rare, is now becoming more and more acceptable, but again there is no specific data relating to widows. De facto polygyny, sanctioned and unsanctioned, is probably already widespread. In Harlem, New York, there is such an acute shortage of black Mus-lim males that the authorities 'now turn a blind eye [to the fact] that most resident males have several wives' seeing this as the best solution to the problem (Morris, 1997). But how prevalent this is amongst widows is not known.

Intimacy.

Many gerontologists have concluded that the deprivation of intimacy in age contributes greatly to physical and psychological decline.

Deprivation of intimacy is a major problem in widowhood because in modern life spouses are usually the only source of adult intimacy for each other.

Given the statistics of divorce and widowhood today, these considerations should lead us to question whether coupling should remain the only answer to intimacy. With the extended years of age, may not the investment of intimacy in one 'significant other', for which we are socialised in our culture from infancy, be too risky, especially for women? Would it not be more prudent to have several intimate people in our lives, both physically and psychologically? Perhaps extended families, adopted families, polygamous families or open marriages would be better suited to our times.

Paradoxically, studies are revealing that some older people of both sexes often feel less lonely than in their youth. I remember noticing an increased ease in and hunger for, expanding intimacies in my own mother as friends and relations began to die off during her later years. She seemed to make friends more easily instead of less, as I always believed to happen with advancing age. She lost her fear and distaste for dogs and cats and cultivated intimacy with tradesmen, inviting them to stay to lunch or run her errands. In age, her network of affectionate people was in strong contrast to the restricted circle of trusted friends which characterised my childhood.

Similarly, even though a majority of widows report loneliness as the major problem of widowhood (Lopata, 1987), many also report feeling less lonely in some ways than when they were still married and confined to intimacy only with their husbands. Widowhood had forced them to develop closer relationships with a wider variety of people. These reports need closer investigation.

Adaptability.

New research has revealed that many older women adjust to the death of a spouse and, with whatever grief or pain, move on to new strengths with less difficulty than younger women - or men at any age (Friedan, 1997).

Mortality rates for widowers rise sharply in the first two years of widowhood but drop if they remarry. No such drastic toll takes place with widows (mortality rates for widows and married women are the same).

This strength of older women to create a new life, to redefine themselves in later life needs to be researched, then results put to use in preparation for widowhood.

The cross-over effect.

'Many widows report strong feelings of inadequacy and incompetence because of their inability to handle money transactions or maintain an automobile. Widows feel very unfeminine doing things previously undertaken by the husband' (Lopata, 1973). Filling the car with petrol became the major issue in my adaptation to widowhood.

As we had only one car during my married life, I never filled the car with gas. Without any specific agreement on the matter, my husband had simply seen to it whenever the gas indicator was low. I learnt to fill the gas tank of my car in 30 seconds after my husband died. But it took over a year for me to shed my feelings of deprivation at having no male to do this trivial chore for me as other women had. I now watch women sitting smugly in the passenger seats of cars at gas stations while their husbands fill the tank, as I once did. Incidentally, I realise only now that I seldom see men sitting there while their wives fill the tank. It seems to be a lingering male role of which I was completely unaware until I lost my husband. Nor did I feel any emotional warmth or comfort sitting in the passenger seat while he filled the tank. I was probably bored. Yet the lack of a man to carry out this task upset me for months after David died.

I learnt to read a bank statement, to juggle bank accounts, to cover periodic payments of mortgages, or automatic withdrawals by gas and fuel and electricity companies, to change a light bulb and check the fire alarms, to buy new motor car--- just about everything that David had previously been responsible for-- far quicker than I learnt to stop feeling demeaned and unloved and all because for the first time in my life I was caring for myself.

Widowhood forces women to assume tasks and roles previously carried out by the husband and widows report this as a stressful, psychologically painful consequence of widowhood. However, for couples who survive into their later years, it now seems that a 'cross-over' in sex roles occurs. 'Once the child-rearing years are over, couples find themselves with an 'empty nest' and many women start to look to the outer world for more education, careers, jobs - the type of lives their husbands had experienced, while many men go off in search of younger wives and a new family in which they seek out a more nurturing role in the home and in child-rearing. It is as if the suppressed masculinity of women and femininity of men will out to find expression, in the last phase of life' (Friedan, 1997).

Widows, instead of feeling pain and loss of status in the necessity of undertaking traditional male roles in widowhood, might see their situation as a bonus in this regard if the 'cross-over' effect of aging were more widely understood in the community. If this 'cross-over' in age is real, then it could be a great bonus in widowhood for just at the time when women are experiencing this surge of power and hunger for self-assertion and independence they are most likely to become widowed. However, just when they most need to see themselves as capable of acquiring independence, they are hit with the loss of confidence and self-esteem which usually accompanies widowhood. Aided and abetted by society's image of widows, they see themselves as losing legitimacy as women, rather than achieving the independence of the cross-over effect of the later years of life.

This blocking of a natural personality development can have severe effects. More and more today, depression is being shown to underlie many of the physical ailments of age and depression itself is often the outcome of unbearable rage turned against oneself. The blocking of a natural personality development as, for example, the repression of sexuality in adolescents by an overly strict religious upbringing, will cause frustration, which in turn will cause inner rage and hence depression and physical illness.

We know a great deal about the development of personality in the earlier stages of the human life cycle - from infancy to childhood to adolescence to adulthood. Our denial of aging has caused us to neglect the study of personality development in age. But there is no reason to doubt that this is as real and as urgent as in the earlier stages of life.

Once again we are in terra incognita as people live longer and longer. But it seems plausible to assume that if widowhood did not incur social delegitimisation it might, in fact, aid the sexual cross-over in later life for women as it necessitates the shedding of dependency and the growth of self-sufficiency. Study of psychological phenomena such as this would help to reduce much unnecessary suffering and self-doubt and open the way to quicker and fuller growth and development of the latent talents of widows.

Widowhood as adventure.

Before widowhood can ever become a positive experience, we must open our minds to the possibility that it could be so, that change could happen, that widowhood could be an adventure.

I was once startled by the remark of an elderly gentleman that 'all the widows he knows seem to come alive after their husbands die'. I have no doubt that he was being exposed to a biased sample of widows. Nonetheless, it alerted me to the possibility that I too may be encountering an equally biased sample. I have certainly met many widows who have triumphed over the ordeal of losing their husbands, but on the whole my impression is that most don't.

The burning question then becomes why can some widows not only survive reasonably well but actually flourish in widowhood, when so many do not?

The catalyst needed to see a situation in a new way, or to recognise new potentials in yourself is often triggered by some shocking event that throws you into total chaos. If you can stay with the pain, something may eventually emerge from that distress that can lead you to a new way of understanding and living. This experience was superbly illustrated in the case-history of an artist who, as a result of a head injury, lost all colour vision and even the ability to recall colour in his imagination (Oliver Sacks, The Case of the Colour- Blind Man 1987). In the beginning he was devastated; he found himself in a world without hope, a world in which for him the lights had gone out. He went through the expected process of mourning and depression. But then, one day when driving to work very early, he saw the sun rise – a black blob which he dubbed a nuclear sun, coming up on the horizon. He was profoundly moved by the association and painted the experience call-ing his work 'The Nuclear Sunrise'. He suddenly realised that he had seen something that no other person had ever seen the same way before. When he was subsequently offered the benefit of a discovery which might restore his colour vision, he refused the treatment. He had, by force, stayed with his pain, worked through his grief, accepted the loss and then moved on to grow with it.

Nothing could better describe my feelings once I realised that I had emerged from the tunnel of my grief and despite myself, ac-cepted the unacceptable and in so doing, became a different person from the one that had entered it.

Changes in personality that lead to the acceptance of radically new life situations and vice versa, should be researched for a better understanding of how to help widows to see their new potentials in widowhood.

Intergenerational strife.

The growing costs of medical care of the aged engenders a dan-gerous potential for intergenerational conflict.

What are the repercussions for widows likely to be as it be-comes progressively more evident that most of those responsible for the medical tax blow-out are likely to be not only women but also widows?

If we don't now create a social infrastructure for widows to achieve independence, society may soon not only denigrate wid-ows but also turn hostile towards them. The psychological threat that widows present to society because of their social and sexual ambiguity will be further aggravated by economic concerns as their numbers continue to increase, as happened before in early Christian and feudal times.

Inter-gender strife.

Among the many unstudied aspects of the new problems of widowhood is the psychological reaction of males to the fact that their wives are now outliving them in such huge numbers. How do men feel knowing in advance that probably their wives will ultimately have control of everything they accumulate together in their marriage? And how will this further be complicated by the increasing incidence of second marriages in which widows will be left administering the inheritance of children of their late husband's previous marriages? How will husbands feel if their wives endeavour to prepare themselves in advance for widowhood? With the increasing invocation of 'living wills', how do men feel about appointing their younger wives as their legal representatives in the decision on when to 'pull the plug' by stopping life supporting treatment in the event of their being unable to make such a decision for themselves? A significant part of the mythology of widows already embodies the notion that they are in some way responsible for their husband's deaths. (It will be recalled that in medieval Europe, the growing inheritance rights of widows to their husbands' estates were finally curbed because it was feared they might become an inducement to wives to kill their husbands!)

This is an area requiring immediate and serious investigation.

Appendix II: Prepare for widowhood

L ike motherhood, retirement and other passages of life, widowhood can be made easier by planning proactively. Most of what is suggested in this list must be started long before the onset of widowhood, as the dysfunctional role of women in widowhood can best be corrected before widowhood begins.

Start to do a little of everything that is gender divided in your household.

- Write checks for gas and electricity, or arrange for automatic payments by the bank
- Change a light bulb
- Fix a fuse
- Relight the boiler
- Fill the car with gas
- Read a road map

You don't have to take over any of these roles - just get a little practice. It will save a great deal of anguish one day.

Expand your circle of friends to include more singles.

Singles often live less structured, more spontaneous lives than married couples – Margaret Mead pointed out that married couples could expand their horizons by including singles amongst their

friends. Single seniors crave the social acceptability amongst couples in our couple- oriented society. The best friendships result
from those offering mutual benefit to both parties. Having an established circle of single friends will be an enormous boost at the
onset of widowhood.

Increase your non-couple specific activities.

Invest time in developing non-couple specific interests with
married friends during married life. E.g., hiking, birdwatching,
bowling, book discussion groups, adult education classes - activities additional to those usually restricted to couples, such as dinner
parties, social bridge for couples or couple holidays and overseas
travel. Women who have had non-couple based interests with their
married friends will be less isolated by the social restructuring imposed by the rupture of the husband-wife bond.

Be involved in every aspect of home economics.

Many widows find taking over the business affairs, such as insurance, banking and debts, a daunting experience of widowhood.
.Practice ahead of widowhood forcing you to take over these duties will save much anguish at a time when you will be least able
to cope with it.

Learn to think about widowhood in financial terms.

Explore the available possibilities for providing for widowhood.

Mortgage insurance (against death of either breadwinner)

Adequate superannuation (currently predominantly a male domain only)

Life insurance for the major provider (currently viewed mainly in relation to dependent children and not the expanding years of widowhood)

Be aware of special Social Security rules (eg., widow benefits are only payable to divorcees who were married for 10 years or more. This is particularly important when there are children still to be reared).

Even with the rapidly expanding involvement of women in the work force, women in general experience a loss of income in widowhood.

Plan a new occupation

 For the time when you will have no-one but yourself to be responsible for, just as people today plan for early retirement by cultivating new skills and hobbies before they retire.

Increase the number of activities you do alone

I always went to lectures alone and found no psychological problem continuing to do so in widowhood. But I never went to the movies alone and still cannot go in widowhood, yet I have friends who do and love it. I cannot eat in a restaurant by myself, yet my stepdaughter treats herself to meals out alone. Above all, start to cultivate inner resources for time alone - some people can't do without it.

Start to learn about loneliness.

Read books about this subject. Loneliness is today a well-studied phenomenon, both psychologically and physiologically. It is devastating on both counts. It can be alleviated and even sublimated with education.

People can be lonely in any situation (including marriage), in a crowd, with friends and so this topic is relevant to all people. It is especially significant in widowhood, as loneliness is usually ranked top of the list of the problems of widowhood by widows themselves.

Widen your circle of emotional intimacy.

Those with several intimate friends can cope with the loss of their lifetime partners much better than those for whom the spouse was the only intimate adult friend.

Befriend widows

Ask widows you know about widowhood and learn from them what they will tell you you need to do to prepare for widowhood. And when the time comes this will provide a circle of unique friends who will be the only ones who really understand what you are experiencing.

Enlist a friend

Just as it is customary today to enlist a friend or husband to help one through the birthing process, one can enlist a friend to help you (or each other) through the grieving process. In severe bereavement, one-to-one support is needed for a protracted period, usually one to two years.

Practice empathising with a widow

Think 'there but for the grace of God go I' and think what you can do to change the social stigmatisation and marginalisation of widows, because one day you will reap the benefit of such change.

Plan a retirement commune

Plan group retirement living with an eye to the needs and compatibility of the wives of the couples involved, as these are the ones who will eventually rely on each other for companionship and intimacy.

Appendix III: A guide for widows

You have an obligation to make the most and not the least of life for as long as you have it.

Do not view the present as a continuation of the past. Nothing stands still. Always remember that, had your husband lived, life would not have been simply more of what it was before he died - he might have become chronically ill, he might have left you for a younger woman (more and more do in this gender lopsided era), he may have developed Alzheimer's disease, he may have won the lottery but he may also have become a compulsive gambler; he would probably have deteriorated mentally and physically at a faster rate than you.

Each phase of life is a discrete experience and there is no reason that widowhood should not be one such phase, defined by its own possibilities and limitations, independent of the phase that preceded it.

Count the ways in which you have benefited from widowhood and then add one each day until you have absolutely exhausted the possibilities. When you have reached ten, aim for fifteen; when you reach fifteen, aim for twenty. The very search will enhance your life.

Be proud of your new status - you are a survivor of one of life's greatest trials. Widowhood is as much a milestone in life as adolescence, adulthood, marriage and motherhood; to live it positively and productively is an achievement.

Do not be an accomplice in the denigration of widowhood. *Do not aid those who seek to degrade you by feeling degraded.*

Do not be an accomplice in the denial of widowhood. *Proclaim your widowhood with pride. Do not help others to avoid their discomfort with your existence, but rather endeavour to help them to face it by promoting the issues of widowhood rather than hiding them.*

Do not be an accomplice in the marginalisation of widows *by becoming invisible. Identify with widows, join widow-to-widow groups, lobby politicians on widow issues, stand for parliament on a widow's ticket, do anything you like but do not move off centre stage.*

Consciously counter the stigma of widowhood:

> *Associate publicly with widows*

> *Speak freely of your own widowhood*

Identify yourself with confidence - ***'I am a widow'*** *- until you are no longer aware of yourself as different from any other woman. It comes with practice, just as a newlywed needs to practice the new title 'Mrs.' until it sounds natural or displays her ring until it becomes part of her.*

Be politically aware of your own interests as a widow.

Widows are marginalised, denigrated and economically disadvantaged by society today. This can only be changed by consciousness-raising by widows themselves of other widows and society at large. Talk to other widows, form self-help groups, network with other such groups. Set the wheels of political action in motion. Widows, who were among the first disadvantaged groups given Divine recognition, are amongst the last remaining ones denied social recognition.

Remember you are not alone *- more than half the women alive today will share your experience of widowhood.*

Appendix IV: TABLES

Table 1	Percentage of Australian population who are widowed by age (2016)	
Age	% Widows[a]	% Widowers[b]
50	2	<1
60	5.8	1.8
65	16.9	4.6
75	41.8	12.5
>85	74	33

Notes: [a]% of all adult females (ie. over 15 years of age). [b]% of all adult males (ie. over 15 years of age).

Source: Australian Bureau of Statistics, (2016)

Table 2	Australian Gender ratios[a] (1881-2016)	
Year	Total Population	Widowhood
1881	128.5	61.4
1891	124.7	59.9
1901	114.7	53.4
1911	110.5	49.9
1921	103.4 (WWI)	-
1947	100.4(WWII)	36.2
1954	102.4	32.2
1976	100.4	28.4
1985	99.7	22.0
1995	97.6	24.6
1996	95.9	23.5
2016	97.4	27.1

Note: Number of men to every 100 women. If more than 100, there is a surplus of men; if less than 100, there is a shortage of men.

In 1881 there were 3 widowers to every 5 widows.

In 1996 there was 1 widower to every 5 widows.

Even when there were more men than women in the total population, there were still more widows than widowers.

Table 3   Absolute numbers of Australian widows and widowers by age and gender.

Year	15 Years		65 Years +		Excess of Widows		% of Widows	Female/Male Ratio	Gender Ratio		Total Population	% of Total Population	
	Widowers	Widows	Widowers	Widows	15 Years +	65 Years +	65 Years +		15 +	65 +		Widowers (65+)	Widows (65+)
1881	31 000	50 000	9000	12 000	19 000	3000	24.0	1.6	62	75	-	-	-
1891	47 000	79 000	15 000	22 000	32 000	7000	27.8	1.6	59	68	-	-	-
1901	57 000	107 000	22 000	39 000	50 000	17 000	36.4	1.8	53	56	-	-	-
1911	64 000	128 000	26 000	54 000	64 000	28 000	42.2	2.0	50	48	4 400 000	1.45 (0.59)	2.91(1.27)
1947	112 000	309 000	-	-	197 000	-	-	2.8	36	-	-	-	-
1954	116 000	351 000	-	-	235 000	-	-	3.0	32	-	-	-	-
1961	116 000	409 000	68 000	241 000	293 000	173 000	58.9	3.5	28	28	-	-	-
1976	134 000	576 000	-	-	442 000	-	-	4.2	23	-	-	-	-
1981	139 000	622 000	-	-	483 000	-	-	4.5	22	-	-	-	-
1985	143 000	649 000	-	-	506 000	-	-	4.5	22	-	-	-	-
1990	160 000	678 000	-	-	518 000	-	-	4.2	24	-	-	-	-
1991	165 000	681 000	-	-	516 000	-	-	4.5	22	-	-	-	-
1992	167 000	685 000	-	-	518 000	-	-	4.1	24	-	-	-	-
1993	167 000	690 000	-	-	523 000	-	-	4.1	24	-	-	-	-
1994	171 000	694 000	-	-	523 000	-	-	4.1	25	-	-	-	-
1995	173 000	698 000	-	-	525 000	-	-	4.1	25	-	-	-	-
1996	171 000	727 000	133 000	576 000	556 000	443 000	79.2	4.3	24	23	17 900 000	0.95(0.74)	4.06(3.22)
2016	210 000	774 000	170 000	647 000	564 000	477 000	83.6	5.1	27	26	19 000 000	1.10	4.07

Notes: At the beginning of the twentieth century, there were 2 widows to every widower; at the end of the twentieth century, there are 4 widows to every widower.

The percentage of the female population widowed increased by 40% during the twentieth century while the percentage of the male population widowed decreased by 52.6%. The percentage of widows over the age of 65 steadily increased from approximately 25% to 80% during this century as the total population aged.

The female/male ratio appears to have stabilised at a level of 4 widows to every widow. Similarly, the gender ratio fell from around 50 widowers to every 100 widows at the beginning of the twentieth century to 25 widowers to every 100 widows at the end of the twentieth century. The gender ratio is remarkably similar amongst those widowed young (before 65) and the older widowed population, showing that either men have a higher mortality rate across all ages, or they remarry at even higher rates when widowed young.

The female/male ratio amongst the widowed population increased steadily until the 1970's. It appears to have stabilised since then at the level of 4 widows to each widower. This suggests that the gap between the increasing medical benefits to ageing women over men has ceased to widen in the last two and a half decades.

Table 4   Excess of widows over widowers in Australia (thousands)(ABS 2016)

	Difference between numbers of widows and widowers	Increase in excess from previous year
1947	198	-
1954	238	40
1961	293	54
1976	442	149
1982	480	48
1987	513	23
1992	528	15
1996	542	11
2016	565	23

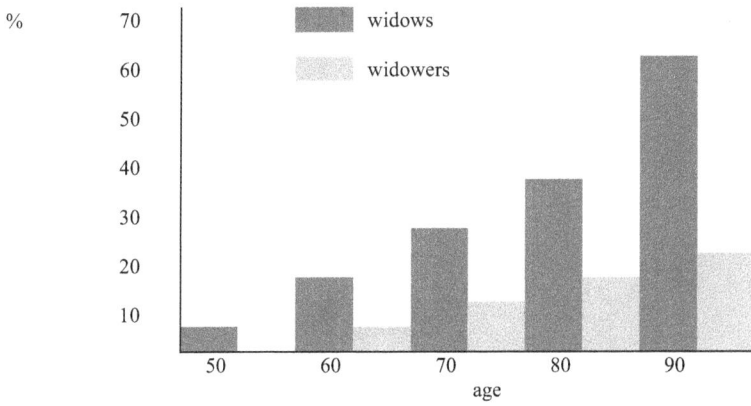

Figure 1: Percentage of Australian population widowed by age (1996)
Notes: The percentage of women widowed to men widowed increased with age over the last century.
Source: ABS, 1996

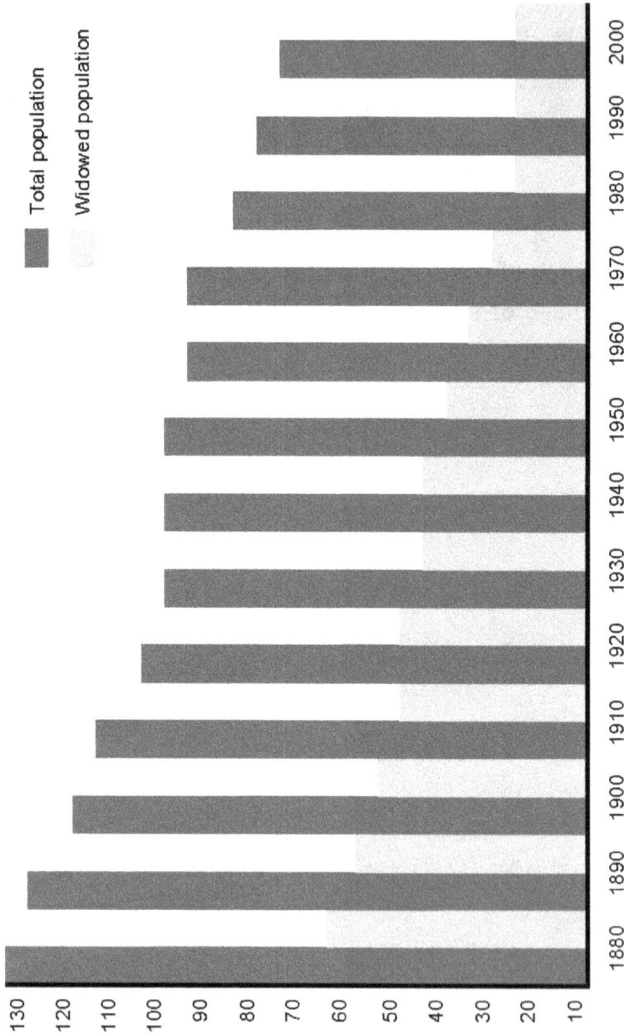

Figure 2 Australian gender ratio (1880-2000)

Notes: The gender ratio of the widowed population decreased more than for the total population during the twentieth century.

Source: ABS, 1996

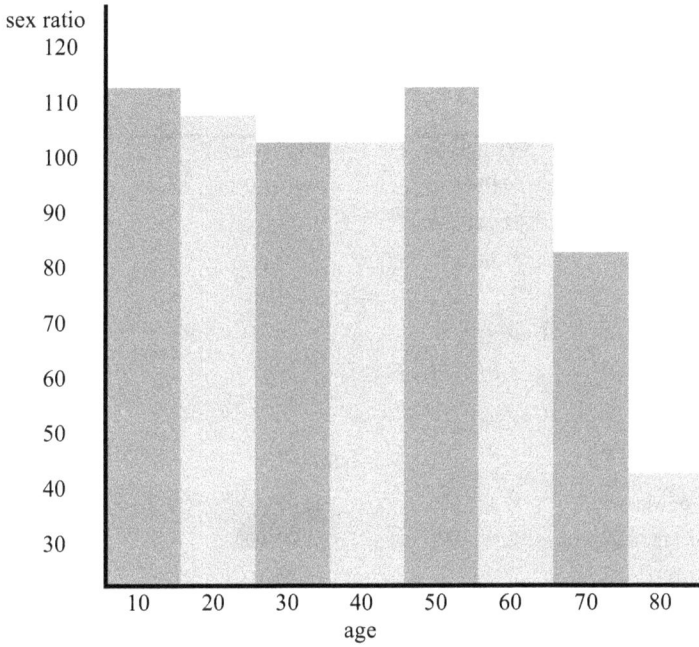

Figure 3   **Australian sex ratios by age (1993)**

Notes: Negative sex ratios begin to appear around 65 years of age.
Source: ABS, 1996

Table 5   Demographics of widowhood in the USA

	1990 (15+)	1996 (15+)	1998 (18+)
Total population	193 368 000	204 625 000	197 412 000
no of women	99 624 000	106 031 000	102 403 000
no. of men	93 744 000	98 593 000	95 009 000
sex ratio	94.1	93.0	92.8
% of women widowed	12.2	10.4	10.8
% of men widowed	2.5	2.5	2.7
Widowed Population			
no. of widows	12 127 000	11 078 000	11 027 000
no. of widowers	2 311 000	2 478 000	2 567 000
sex ratio	19.1	22.4	

Source: US Bureau of the Census.

| Table 6 | Differences in male and female life expectancies in countries with life expectancies under 60 years |

Country	Population	Life Expectancy		Difference
	(millions)	Males	Females	(years)
Afghanistan	19	43.00	44.00	1
Angola	11	44.90	48.10	3
Benin	5	45.92	49.29	3
Burkina	10	45.84	49.01	3
Burundi	6	48.42	51.92	3
Camaroon	13	54.50	57.50	3
Bangladesh	117	56.91	55.97	(reversal) 1
Ivory coast	14	49.69	52.38	3
Ethiopia	55	45.93	49.06	3
Ghana	17	54.22	57.84	4
Guatemala	10	55.11	59.43	4
Guinea	7	44.00	45.00	1
Haiti	7	54.95	58.34	3
India	919	57.70	58.10	0
Iran	59	58.38	59.70	1
Kenya	29	54.18	57.29	3
Laos	5	49.50	52.50	3
Liberia	3	45.80	44.00	(reversal) 2
Madagascar	14	55.00	58.00	3
Malawi	9	43.51	46.75	3
Mali	10	55.24	58.66	3
Mozambique	17	44.88	48.01	3
Myanmar	46	57.89	63.14	5
Nepal	21	50.88	48.10	(reversal) 3
Niger	9	44.90	48.14	3
Nigeria	108	44.81	52.01	3
Pakistan	127	59.04	59.20	0
Papua	4	55.16	56.16	1
Russia	148	58.91	71.88	13!
Rwanda	8	45.10	47.70	3
Senegal	8	48.30	50.30	2
Sierra Leone	4	37.47	40.58	3
Somalia	9	45.41	48.60	3
Sudan	29	51.58	54.37	3
Tanzania	29	47.00	50.00	3
Togo	4	53.23	56.82	4
Uganda	21	43.57	46.19	3
Yemen	16	49.90	50.40	0
Zambia	9	50.70	53.00	2
Zimbabwe	11	58.00	62.00	4

Notes: Average difference in life expectancy between men and women is 2 years.

Table 7

Differences in male and female life expectancies in countries with life expectancies between 60 and 70 years

Country	Population	Life Expectancy		Difference
	(millions)	Males	Females	(years)
Albania	3	69.60	75.50	6
Algeria	27	65.75	66.34	1
Argentina	34	68.17	73.09	5
Armenia	3	68.66	75.51	7
Belarus	10	64.92	75.45	10!
Bosnia-Herzegovina	3	69.55	75.11	7
Brazil	153	64.04	68.68	5
Bulgaria	8	67.61	74.39	7
Chile	14	68.54	75.59	7
China	1209	66.70	70.45	4
Colombia	35	66.36	72.26	6
Croatia	5	68.29	75.63	7
Czechoslovakia	10	69.28	76.35	7
Egypt	59	62.86	66.39	3
Georgia	5	68.10	75.70	7
Honduras	6	65.43	70.06	5
Hungary	10	64.53	73.81	9
Indonesia	192	61.00	64.50	3
Jordan	5	66.16	69.84	4
Kazakhstan	17	63.83	73.06	9
North Korea	23	67.70	73.95	6
South Korea	45	67.66	75.67	8
Kyrgyzstan	5	64.60	72.74	8
Libya	5	61.58	65.00	3
Malaysia	20	68.68	73.04	4
Mexico	93	62.10	66.00	4
Molodova	4	64.28	70.99	7
Morocco	27	61.58	65.00	3
Nicaragua	4	64.8	67.71	3
Paraguay	5	66.30	70.83	4
Peru	23	62.77	66.56	4
Philippines	67	63.10	66.70	4
Poland	39	66.11	75.27	9
Romania	23	66.56	73.17	6
Saudi Arabia	17	68.39	71.41	3
Slovakia	5	66.64	75.44	9
Sri Lanka	18	67.78	71.66	4
Tajikistan	6	66.80	71.70	5
Thailand	61	63.82	68.85	5
Tunisia	9	66.85	68.68	2
Turkey	61	63.26	66.01	3
Ukraine	52	66.14	75.17	9
Uzbekistan	21	66.00	72.10	6
Venezuela	21	66.68	72.80	6
Yugoslavia	11	69.50	74.49	5

Notes: Average difference in life expectancy between men and women is 5 years.

Table 8 Differences in male and female life expectancies in countries with life expectancies over 70 years

Country	Population	Life Expectancy		Difference
	(millions)	Males	Females	(years)
Australia	18	74.99	80.86	6
Austria	8	72.87	79.35	6
Belgium	10	72.43	79.13	7
Canada	29	73.02	79.79	7
Costa Rica	3	72.89	77.60	5
Cuba	11	72.89	76.80	4
Denmark	5	72.35	77.78	5
Finland	5	70.93	78.87	8
France	58	72.91	81.13	8
Germany	81	71.81	78.38	6
Italy	57	73.50	80.03	7
Greece	10	74.61	79.96	5
Japan	125	76.25	82.51	6
Holland	15	74.21	80.20	6
New Zealand	3	72.86	78.74	6
Norway	4	74.24	80.25	6
Portugal	10	70.77	78.01	7
Spain	39	73.40	80.49	7
Sweden	9	75.49	80.79	5
Switzerland	7	74.70	81.40	7
USA	265	72.00	78.90	7
UK	79	72.20	79.40	7

Notes: Average difference in life expectancy between men and women is 6 years.

Female life expectancies are higher than male in almost every country in the world, even where the influence of modern medical care is minimal.

Women are living progressively longer than men as life expectancies rise.

In Table 6 – countries with life expectancies under 60 years - the average difference is 2.1 years.

In Table 7 - countries with life expectancies between 60 and 70 years - the average difference is 5.9 years.

In Table 8 – countries with life expectancies over 70years – the average difference is 6.6 years.

Enormous differences in male and female life expectancies (those over 9 years) are due to some extraordinary prevalent factor such as local wars, epidemic male alcoholism in the countries of the former Soviet Republic, etc. These have been excluded from these calculations.

Source: Figures for Tables 6-8 taken from Whitaker's Almanack, The Stationary Office: London,1998.

Bibliography

Abrams, M.H. ed 1986 The Norton Anthology of English Literature
5th edition W.W. Norton, New York

Anderson, B.S. and Zinsser, J 1988 A History of Their Own. Penguin,
Harmondsworth, UK

Australian Bureau of Statistics (ABS) 1995 Marriages and Divorces,
ABS, Canberra

Badinter, E. 1981 The Myth of Motherhood, Souvenir Press, London

Barnard, J. 1972 The Future of Marriage, Penguin Books, New York

Baron, SW 1952 Ancient Times, Columbia Press, New York

Barron, C.M. and Sutton, A.F. eds. 1994 Medieval London Widows
(1380-1500), Hambledon Press, London

Basken, J. 1985 'Women in Rabbinic Judaism' Women, Religion and Social Change eds. Y.Y. Haddad & E.B. Findly, State University of New York Press, Albany, NY

Bernard, J. 1972 The Future of Marriage, Penguin, New York

Bowling, A. and Cartwright, A. 1982 Life After Death, Tavistock Publications, London

Bremmer, J. and Van Bosch, L. eds 1995 Between Poverty and the Pyre: Moments in the History of Widowhood, Routledge, New York

Brothers, J. 1990 Widowed Ballantine Books, New York

Caine, L. 1974 Widow, Bantam, Sydney

Carnegie Trust 1993 Carnegie Inquiry into the Third Age Research Paper No.3, The Carnegie Trust, London

Cherfas, J. and Gribbin, J. 1983 The Redundant Male, Pantheon Books, New York

Clements, M. 1999 The Improvised Woman: Single Women Reinventing Single Life, W.W. Norton, London

Cline, S. 1995 Lifting the Taboo, Little Brown, Boston, MA

Cohen, J.M. and Cohen, M.J. eds 1960 The Penguin Dictionary of Quotations, Penguin Books, Harmondsworth, UK

Davis Ginsberg, G. 1987 To Live Again, Bantam, Los Angeles

DiGiulio, R.C. 1989 Beyond Widowhood, MacMillan, New York

Fergusson, R. 1983 The Penguin Dictionary of Proverbs, Allen Lane, London

French, M. 1992 The War Against Women, Summit Books, New York

Friedan, B. 1994 The Fountain of Age, Vintage, London

Gies, F. and Gies, J. 1980 Women in the Middle Ages, Barnes & Noble, New York

Gottman, J. 1994 Why Marriages Fail, Simon Schuster, New York

Greer, G. 1999 The Whole Woman, Transworld, London

----1991 The Change: Women, aging and the Menopause, Hamish
Hamilton Press, London

Guttenberg, M. and Secord, P. 1983 Too Many Women, Sage, Los
Angeles

Hackett, R. 1985 'Women and Religious Plurality in Nigeria'
Women, Religion and Social Change eds. Y.Y. Haddad &
E.B. Findly, State University of New York Press, Albany, NY

Hafner, J. 1993 The End of Marriage: Why Monogamy Isn't Working, Century, London

Harvey, P.D.A. 1965 A Medieval Oxfordshire Village: Cuxham 1240-
1400, Oxford University Press, Oxford

Hite, S. 1987 The Hite Report on Love, Passion and Emotional Violence, Alfred A. Knopf Inc., New York

----1987 The Hite Report on Male Sexuality, Alfred A. Knopf Inc.,
New York

Hochschild, A 1973 The Unexpected Community, Prentice Hall, Englewood Cliffs, NJ

Holmes, T.H. and Rahe, R.H. 1967 'The Social Readjustment Rating Scale' Journal of Psychosomatic Research, vol. 11 no. 2, PP. 213-218

Holt, P. 1999 Stars of India: Travels in Search of Astrologers and Fortune Tellers, Trafalgar Square, London

Johnson, P. 1996 The Quest for God: A Personal Pilgrimage, Harper Collins, London

Lawlor, R. 1991 Voices of the First Day: Awakening in the Aboriginal Dreamtime, Inner Traditions International, Rochester, VT

Lieberman, M. 1996 Doors Open, Doors Close, Putnam, New York

Lopata, H Z. 1973 Widowhood in an American City Schenker, Cambridge, MA

----1979 Women as Widows, Elsevier, New York

----1987 Widows in North America, Duke University Press, NY

----1996 Current Widowhood – Myths and Realities, Sage, London

McKenzie M., Pettepas, M and Wilson, E 1974 Helping each Other in Widowhood, Health Services Publishing Corp., New York

McNeill Taylor, L. 1983 Living with Loss, Fontana, London

Mills, J. 1991 Woman Words, Virago, London

Mirrer, L. ed 1992 Upon My Husband's Death, Ann Arbor University Press, Ann Arbor, Mikey

Morris, D. 1997 The Human Sexes: A Natural History of Man and Woman, Network Books, London

Morton, T. 1997 Altered Mates, Allen & Unwin, Melbourne

Murdock, C.P. 1967 Ethnographic Atlas, University of Pittsburg Press, Pittsburg, PA

Partington, A. ed 1996 <u>Oxford Concise Dictionary of Quotations</u>, Oxford University Press, Oxford

Pifer, A. and Bronte, L 1986 <u>Our Aging Society</u>, W.W. Norton & Co., New York

Plath, S. 1970 'Widow' <u>Crossing the Water: Transitional Poems</u>, Harper & Collins, London

Pool, N. and Feldman, S. 1999 <u>A Certain Age</u>, Allen & Unwin, StLeonards, NSW

Reuben, David, AnyWoman Can, Bantam Books1976

Rosenman, L. and Shulman, A. 1987 'Widowed Women in Australia' <u>Widows</u> ed H.Z. Lopata, Duke University Press, Durha

Sacks,Oliver,The Case of the Colour-blind Man,1987

Scadron, A. ed 1988 <u>On Their Own: Studies of Widowhood in the American Southwest from 1848 to 1939</u>, University of Illinois Press, Urbana, IL

Schechtman, S.J. 1992 On the Economics of Marriage, Westview Press, Oxford

Scolnick, A.S. 1978 The Intimate Environment, Little Brown, Boston, MA

Sheehy, G. 1995 New Passages, Random House, New York

Silverman, P. ed 1986 Widow-to-Widow, Springer Publishing Co., New York

Sontag, S. 1977 Illness as Metaphor, Farrer, Strauss & Giroux, New York

Stanton, R. 1999 When Your Partner Dies, Allen & Unwin, StLeonards, NSW

Steinem, G. 1992 Revolution from Within: A Book of Self-Esteem, Little Brown, Boston, MA

Toffler, A. 1970 Future Shock, Random House, New York

US Bureau of the Census (USBC) 1993 Marital Status and Living Arrangements, US Government Printing Office, Washington, DC

Vanderbilt, A. 1954 <u>Complete Book of Etiquette: A Guide to Gracious Living</u>, Doubleday, New York

Viney, L.L. 1980 Transitions: <u>The Major Upheavals Most Women Must Face and How They Experience Them</u>, Cassell Australia, North Ryde, NSW

Weisner, M.E. 1986 <u>Working Women in Renaissance Germany</u>, Rutgers University Press, New Brunswick, NJ

Wilson, L. 1992 <u>Life After Death</u>, Temple University Press, Philadelphia

ABOUT THE AUTHOR

Born in Sydney, 1932
Melbourne University, (1952-56 and 1962- 65), BSC degrees psychology
the psycho pathology
Worked in the field of population control for United Nations in Singapore
(1966-68), London School of Hygiene and tropical Medicine (1969-72),
Columbia University, New York (1973-75).
Returned to Australia 1976.
Widowed in 1994

www.ingramcontent.com/pod-product-compliance
Lightning Source LLC
Chambersburg PA
CBHW072226270326
41930CB00010B/2008